The
Universal Energies
of Sacred Sites
with Practical Application

Text and graphics by Sam Holland
Illustrations and Mandalas by Anne Claire Venemans
Cover art by Chris Adkins

computer by iMac
typeset through InDesign
graphics through Photoshop

ISBN 1932101012

We would like to acknowledge all those who have participated in field work with the Records Group. This book is dedicated to them. They are:

Robert Adamson	Lou Nichols
Ron Cantoni	Gary Plapp
Nancy Cassell	Betty Roe
Patrick Corsi	David Ross
Diana Dunckelmann	Shesta Ross
Denise Hall	George Ruby
Jeton Holland	Jim Scheer
Sam Holland	Larry Scheer
Georgia Hughes	Linda Scheer
Lyn Maccarone	Penny Slade
Aram Manukyan	Andrea Smith
Kat Marlowe	Sachi Tatsuma
Archie Mulvena	Anne Claire Venemans
Richard Mynett	

Special thanks to June Burke & Julian for their friendship, patience and their grand ability as a deep trance medium. Thanks also to our etheric friends, Estherelle and Orick.

Contents

Introduction

This book is the outgrowth of work that began in 1976 by a small number of people called the Records Group. The original purpose of this group was to discover and uncover artifacts from the Atlantan era. As the Records Group work progressed we were, through necessity, drawn to a study of how the Earth connects energies with humanity and the Universe.

We found that this connection was accomplished in a way that defined and maintained the purpose of sacred site's. We were amazed at how the Universe is connected to and interacts with everything that is sacred. More amazing still is the multiplicity of sacred site's and their interaction with humanity. The focus of the group eventually became the sacred site's energies and etheric structures that are described in this book.

The Records Group
(left to right top) Shesta Ross, David Ross, Andrea Smith
(bottom) Anne Claire Venemans, Sam Holland

The purpose of this book is to teach you how to create and use a sacred site with strong purpose, longevity and expression. It explains how to use the esoteric energies that are at play, and support the site in a way that is practical. It also describes how to recognize these energies, their purpose and how to use their expression, as well as the details of the Universal energies that are at work in any sacred site. Perhaps more importantly, this book also describes the complex of energies that work together to manifest the energy of every individual sacred site. These descriptions provide a reference manual for fundamental Universal energies.

We feel that it is important to understand the individual energies as well as the multiplicities of their connections. These energies and connections are complex, but if you take them

Introduction

one at a time they provide a grand understanding of how we are connected to the Universe. The intellectual understanding only makes our Universal connection stronger.

We have included a set of cards that depict the energies described in this book. The cards can be used to help create your own customized sacred site, for meditation and study or for divination. These cards, and the details of their energies, are described in Part V of this book.

There is an amazing proliferation of sacred site's. This is due to the fact that the fundamental energies which define a sacred site are also present with every object, place or sentient being. In fact, they are present in everything that needs a connection to the Universe. Who are we to define what is sacred or not? The depersonalized Universe looks at everything as sacred and therefore, is connected to everything.

Many of the energies we have discovered through the use of the tools of dowsing and meditation. Those tools are not described here as they are beyond the scope of this book. However, you can become adept at using those tools through studying many other useful books, taking classes and most importantly, practice. Each of our discoveries has been verified through many avenues. However, they can only become real to you through use and understanding.

This book is divided into a number of parts in order to help break a lot of concentrated information into categories that, more or less, stand on their own.

Part I presents the invisible nature of sacred site's through a description of their energies and etheric structures. It is those energies and structures that give the site's purpose, longevity and interaction. It is also those energies and structures that will help the site, as well as the Earth, move forward into the new vibration at this point of time.

Part II Describes the Earth as a sacred site.

Part III goes into the multiplicity of ways the energies and structures can be of practical use.

Part IV presents a method for using the Universal energies in divination.

Part V defines the details of the Universal energies in a way that makes them available for practical use.

Presenting the energies would serve two purposes.

First, the energies are subdivided into categories that will hopefully help you remember them in a logical way.

Second, through divination, a useful method is shown to use the energies to help you discover answers to all those pressing questions everyone comes across from time to time.

Inherent in the energies, etheric structures and their interconnections are answers to many questions. Including:

What is the basis of astrology?

How do the pressure points and meridians of the body interact with health and well being?

Why does one site feel different than another?

What is the connection between human thought and actions with Earth changes?

What draws me to a particular site or area?

Of course, some study is necessary to find the answers!

In addition, the information presented in this book may seem a bit sparse in places. This is because the intent is to provide a concise reference. Research continues and, as time goes on, additional information and clarified descriptions can be provided.

Meditation was used extensively to discover and understand the energies and etheric structures Therefore, meditation can help the reader to understand and work with the book. The meditative technique used needs to be highly interactive. The energies are living things and need interaction to communicate.

Part I Energy of Sacred Sites

Over the years we have discovered that anything and everything is a sacred site. The following chapters hopefully will delineate these discoveries and help to understand just what makes up a sacred site.

Sacred Sites

When we began our search we assumed that sacred sites were relatively rare, confined, and in isolated places like meditation rooms, temples and churches. Later, we were astounded to find that the energies that make up a sacred site occur in enormous numbers. There are literally dozens of significant sacred sites in a typical home or work place. Yes, some sacred sites are invisible except to the most finely tuned senses, while others, such as a well-used chapel, have energies that are strong and can be easily felt. A meditation Space has a feeling of calmness, where the more chaotic, yet still sacred energy of a food preparation area is easier to find through the sensitivity of dowsing. Both have the same general energy patterns and differ only in the strength and purpose set to the energy. Both are sacred sites.

What is a Sacred Site

The enormous number of sacred site's exists everywhere you look. The sacred site's are defined, not only by physical appearance, but also by a recognizable collection of etheric energies.

These same energies exist in 5,000 year old stone circles, like Castel Rigg above, or the great Pyramid in Egypt. They also exist in churches, temples and synagogues, independently of their age. We have found the same energies in any artifact or icon such as rings, crosses and cards. Indeed, we have found that every person or sentient being has these energies associated with them. For every unique site the representation of the energies is unique and gives a distinctive feeling or identity, but their construction and components are the same. Furthermore, we found that a sacred site exists with everything that needs a connection to the Universe. It seems that the Universe includes every creation and therefore, every creation has a Universal connection. Perhaps it's time to take a fresh look at the definition of sentient!

Sacred sites have a power, or an energy that can be felt, but usually is not seen. For instance, years ago when I was experiencing a particularly difficult time in my life, I felt a need to enter an old church to spend some quiet moments in contemplation. When I entered the church a sense of calm and well being surrounded me. I immediately felt better and had a knowing that whatever happened it was going to be OK. Years later, I had a similar experience on a trip to England. I felt an urge to visit the White Eagle lodge, which is well known for its healing properties. The primary feature of the lodge is a circular temple that has 12 pillars. The temple is held in great reverence and respect by all its members and visitors. Upon entering this temple I was overwhelmed by an enormous sense of love and peace. I felt energies stronger than I had ever known up to that point in time. The energy of those two sites seems to be different yet unchangeable. The spaces have the ability to perpetuate themselves. They have a power that lasts.

Objects also have unique force and power. An object's power is the expression of its purpose, and its force is the movement of that expression. Power, as we use it here, is not domination, it is an expression that is felt, not seen.

This power was brought home when I became fascinated by the expression of tarot cards and wondered why each card has an individual purpose and energy. There seemed to be an attraction between the energy of the cards, the energy of the question and the energies of the reader, the client and Universal wisdom. Dowsing showed that each card has an energy pattern that is constructed identically to the sacred sites of holy sites. These energy patterns have all the ingredients to define the unique properties of the card, and to maintain and perpetuate their individual properties. In other words, each tarot card has a purpose that gives it a discernible energy and creates its own sacred site. An energy is created that touches and can be touched in a way that allows Universal wisdom to aid in the selection of a card for any particular question we choose to ask. The ramifications of the answer go beyond our mundane ability to see. Even though sacred sites have similar components, they work in a way that uniquely serves many diverse purposes.

Sacred sites exist because there is a need to connect the higher purpose of the Universe with our human desire to understand. We need to tap into a site that has a known purpose and doesn't change too much over time. We create sacred sites because we need stable sites in our lives. We need them because they provide a link to our source and to our Universe. They are our silent friends, providing gentle guidance along our path.

The result of creating and using a sacred site is always connected to our individual spiritual growth and to the Universe. It is our good fortune that these sacred sites are created even when we don't have the foggiest idea as to their existence, or for that matter, their ultimate use. All we do is state or create a need, and the Universe does the rest.

What Makes a Sacred Site Powerful

The power of a sacred site depends on its ability to express its purpose. Power is therefore, expression. This type of power is a depersonalized energy and does not dominate. The power of a sacred site is felt, and cannot be seen other than by the most sensitive eyes or through meditation. Any personality given to a sacred site is actually an expression of the personality-based perspective put upon it by the user. The site doesn't care how it is used, it simply expresses its purpose through energies that have no personality. The power or expression of a sacred site depends upon three factors: use, respect and focus. The picture below of a stupa in Tibet displays these factors with great strength.

Let's look at these factors in detail...

Use

The more a site is used the more powerful it becomes. This can be easily verified by visiting a well-attended place of worship and a similar but derelict site. The well-attended place of worship has a stronger energy than one that has become unused. You may not always like the energy, but its use does make it more powerful. This is because the Universal energies that support a site renew themselves with each visit, at least up to a point. That ultimate power depends on other factors such as respect and focus.

The energies return to their source if a site is not used for an extended period of time. However, the energies can be reinstated if the site is used again. If, for whatever the reason, a site is changed to a new use or re-dedicated to a different purpose, the old energies will dissipate over a short period of time. New energies then begin to build with each use of the new purpose. However, the new purpose will always be built upon the old foundations of it.

Respect

The more a site is respected, the more powerful it becomes. Respect, at the very least, means recognizing and thanking the energies each time the site is used. Even though the energies don't have a personality or need for recognition, they are alive and grow.

The vitality of a site is more clearly felt when the site is used for its dedicated purpose. The site's power growth comes from the recognition that, through use, something happened. Recognition stems from appreciation for the energy expended by the site's users and by the Universe.

Respect is also shown by maintaining an area of protection around the site. A fence around a burial site or a separate room or enclosure around a meditation Space provides protection. If a Space is used for two purposes, such as prayer and play, the energy of both is maintained, but neither can reach its full energy potential.

Gossip diminishes respect. No one likes to be talked about behind their back, particularly when the talk involves a lack of credibility or factual information. Similarly, a sacred site senses the lack of respect given through gossip directed toward it. It's not as though the site's feelings are hurt; after all, it has no ego oriented personality, but gossip demonstrates a lack of respect by the users and the site's power is lowered accordingly.

Focus

Your focus during the preparation and use of a site is important for building the site's power. But, perhaps more importantly, it aids in your ability to gain results from the site's use. Strong focus creates strong intent. Intent supports and recognizes that good comes from interaction between you and the site.

Ritual increases intent and focus through repetition. It's not necessarily the ritual that is important. It is the focus created by the ritual. The site senses the focus and reacts accordingly with more powerful energies.

If your focus involves a judgement, it can block communication and might result in unreliable interaction with the sacred site. This is particularly true if the site is used for purposes it wasn't intended for. Unreliability also creeps in if your focus is on a pre-determined result or concentrated only on the result of the focus. If, however, you are focused on your work in partnership with the sacred site, and are open to new information, beneficial results can be achieved. Partnership implies equal billing for yourself and the sacred site. Both your and the site's energies are equal in the eyes of the Universe. If you have an absolute belief in that equality, hold onto your hat, because great good can come from the power the partnership creates.

In summary, clear Universal interaction comes from a number of etheric structures that exist with every sacred site. These structures cannot be seen by the physical eye but are as real as the physical site itself. The purpose of the site is its expression of its purpose and grows through use, respect and focus.

The Components of a Sacred Site

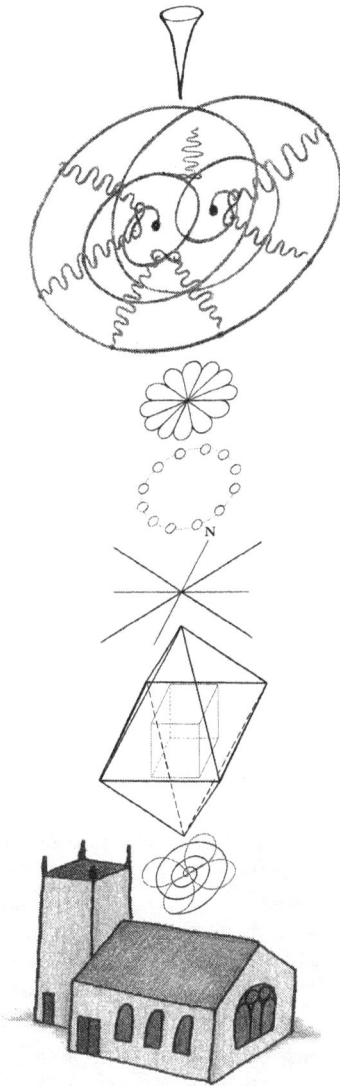

In order to provide and maintain a sacred site, or for that matter, any connection to the Universe, seven components are necessary: motivation (a reason to use it), life force (it needs existence), perpetuation (it needs longevity), formation (it has to manifest the energies), identity (it needs to give us coherent and unique interaction), evolution (it needs to keep up with the times) and memory (it needs a record of its evolution so change is meaningful).

The most important component is the physical object or Space that is built as a result of motivation. Motivation comes from the very philosophical roots of humanity. We are motivated to answer the question: Why are we here and what can we do about it? Those philosophical roots are expressed in sacred site's through an interesting set of etheric components. Without a dedicated physical Space the sacred site cannot exist. Everything else results from a motivation high enough to lead to a physical creation.

Life force, perpetuation, formation, identity, evolution and memory are supported by corresponding etheric structures. These structures cannot be seen by the physical eye but can be found and identified through dowsing. The etheric structures provide the links between the spiritual and the physical worlds. In addition, a flow of energy connects the etheric components, the Universe and the physical sacred site.

Motivation provides the energy to construct and dedicate a physical site.

Life force comes from a Four Pole Magnet and a Spiral that provides a heart beat similar to our human heart.

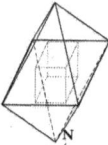

Perpetuation comes from a Pyramid structure that keeps everything anchored in place. Within the Pyramid is a perfect Cube that provides a stable arena for the energies to manifest.

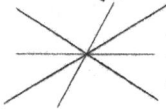

Formation is provided by the four elements, direction and winds.

Identity comes from a petal like complex of energies that interact with a Universal delivery system that stabilizes the site's purpose and allows change to occur.

Evolution comes from what we call a Wisdom Circle that perpetuates Universal energies and stays balanced within Universal law as the site evolves.

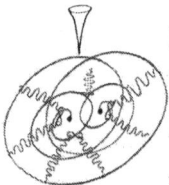

Memory comes from etheric structures that retain the site's essence so the site doesn't deviate from its purpose when significant changes occur. The memory also has an ability to communicate with any other sacred site, including humans.

These seven structures are, in turn, connected to other site's that tie the identities together, not only in the Earth, but throughout the Universe.

Motivation and the Physical Site

Since the beginning of humanity's involvement with the Earth, whenever we felt frustrated or have needed to understand issues that seemed beyond our experience, we have reached upward, toward what we believe to be a greater wisdom. Intuitively we realize that we need something that bridges the spiritual world and the Earth.

We traditionally have done this in a way that expresses our individualism, be it driven by need or by ego. We accomplish this by constructing an Earth-bound icon of some sort, like an altar, temple, church or stone circle. Or, we instill a reverence and respect in an already existing icon such as a grove, a rock or a flower. These site's represent a bridge between our consciousness and the unknown Universe. They represent our respect for what is important to us. For that reason we call them sacred site's.

Motivation falls by the wayside unless a way is found that expresses our creation in a practical, physical way. We need to get involved in a physical activity of some kind. Sometimes we get highly motivated and build huge edifices such as enormous churches. Sometimes we have a need for immediate results and simply rub a stone that we keep in our pocket. We might build a physical representation of the energies in the form of a medicine wheel or stone circle. And sometimes we take a year off and circumambulate Mt. Kailas in Tibet. All of these methods are equally valid as long as the respect and use are there. In other words, we express our motivation through our physical activity, either in the construction of, or through a pilgrimage to, a sacred site.

The physical site is the starting point where everything else follows from the physical site and its purpose. Without the physical anchor, and its visual identity, practicality becomes impossible. Both the physical site and its etheric components are necessary in order to have something that bridges the physical and spiritual worlds.

The Life Force

The Pulse and the Four Pole Magnet

The Four Pole Magnet creates a Pulse that interacts with the sacred site's energies. This Pulse becomes the heart beat of the site much like a human heart regulates the vitality in a human's body. The pulsing action occurs as a result of the Four Pole Magnets movement that include rotation, coupled with a compression and release of the crossing arms. This pulsing action is described in detail in the chapter on Energy Flow.

The Four Pole Magnet is always situated in the center of the sacred site's etheric structures. Other etheric structures within the site use its pulsing action as a source that mixes and moves the site's energies. This means that the Four Pole Magnet is literally the pump that moves the site's life force.

The Spiral

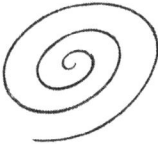

Each site's Four Pole Magnet has a Spiral that winds itself out from the center and then back in upon itself. There are three loops to the Spiral which represent spiritual, mental and physical interaction.

Energy moves through the Spiral in a pulsing manner originating from the Four Pole Magnet. The Pulse moves out to the edge and returns to the center. This motion provides interaction with the rest of the site at the physical, mental and spiritual levels. The movement outward, in a clockwise manner, is the asking. The movement inward, in a counter clockwise manner, is the receiving.

The Laniscate

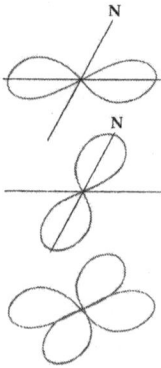

The Laniscate provides a path for etheric energies to interact with physical energies in a way that provides a bridge between the physical and spiritual worlds. The bridging occurs through twelve energies that provide the steps that manifest. Many Laniscates occur in pairs. The Laniscate's energy flows in a receptive or counter clockwise direction in the South or West loops. The energy movement continues in a clockwise or active direction in the North or East loops. Often when dowsing for the etheric structures, many Laniscates are detected. Most them are really echoes of the primary Laniscate at the site's Four Pole Magnet.

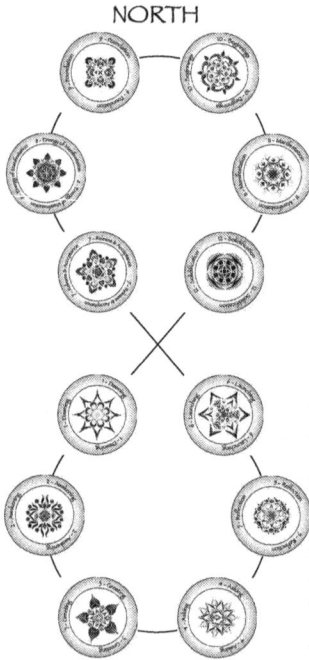

The manifestation path starts by passing through the energies of dawning, awakening, greeting, asking, reflection and launching. The receptive, or counter-clockwise direction of that loop means that the first six stages of manifestation develop a clarity about that which is to be manifested. The second loop of the Laniscate passes through the energies of release and acceptance, energy of manifestation, foundation, beginnings, manifestation and solidification. The clockwise direction of that loop provides the active force that manifests. The North - South aligned Laniscate brings Universal wisdom into a physically useful form. The East -West aligned Laniscate brings the energies into a physically recognized form.

Perpetuation

The Pyramid

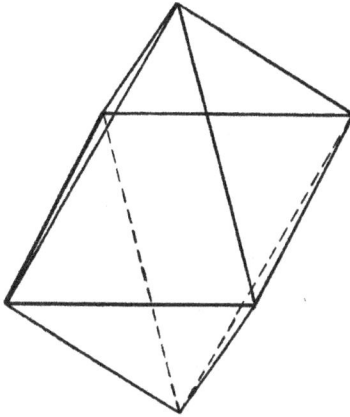

The Pyramid is created by the Universe in response to our need to use the site over an extended period of time. The site's energy is anchored and perpetuated via its Pyramid shaped structure. The Pyramid can be etherically contained within a physical structure, or purely etheric. For instance, roofs or domes of churches provide a Pyramid form that works. Or the Pyramid-like shape of a hill or rock works nicely in natural environments. These physical structures serve to house an etheric Pyramid within them. However, we have found that all site's, particularly those out in the open, have an etheric Pyramid that provides the perpetuation of the energy without the need for a physical Pyramid like structure.

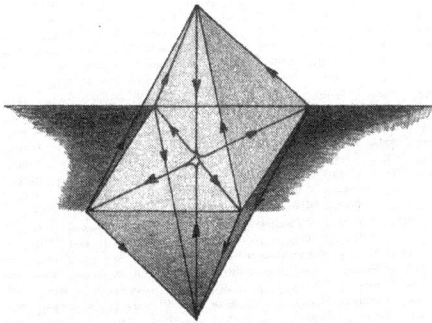

Every Pyramid is like an engine that continually recirculates energy throughout the sacred site so the energy doesn't become stagnant. It's shape provides a framework for the movement of that energy. The energy movement starts at the apex of the Pyramid, then moves down to the center, then spreads out throughout the base back to the sides, then up the sides and back up to the apex. That flow is perpetually repeated. The flow basically mixes the energy that is placed within or fed to the Pyramid.

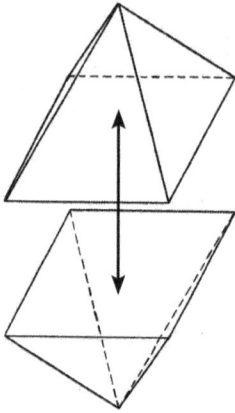

The Pyramid is actually an octahedron that continuously circulates the energy of the spiritual world above and the physical world below. That flow becomes a perpetual movement of energy that serves to anchor the energy at the physical site.

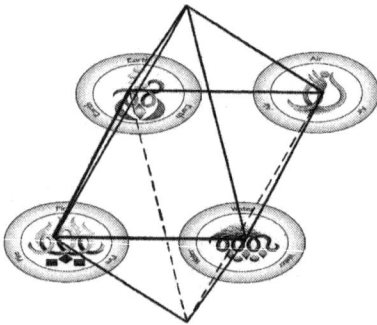

An elemental energy exists at each corner. This placement mixes the energy of earth, water, fire and air with the spiritual (above) and physical (below) worlds. The end result is to circulate and anchor the ingredients necessary to manifest the purpose of the sacred site. This keeps the balance between spiritual wisdom and physical practicability.

The anchored Elemental Energies also are fed into all of the other energies and etheric structures of the site. Thus the stability of the complete site is maintained.

The Cube of Space

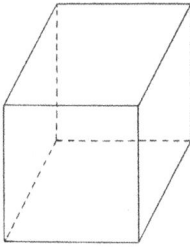

The Cube of Space is a perfect Cube shaped etheric structure. It provides the arena for manifestation to occur and therefore completes the physical - spiritual bridge in consort with the Four Pole Magnet. The Four Pole Magnet rest in the exact center of the Cube. Each part of the Cube is a component of the cycle of growth that relates to humanity or, for that matter, to anything that is manifested. The Cube can be thought of as a halfway house between the spiritual world and the physical world. The origin energies of the Cube of Space are described in many esoteric texts and are usually correlated with the Tarot's 22 major arcana cards and the Kabbalah. Dowsing has shown that there are four additional components of the Cube.

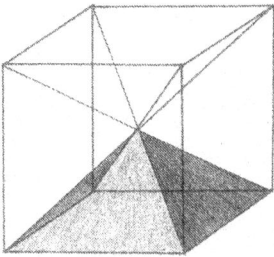

The additions include the corners of the Cube connected by four diagonals. That division forms six inwardly facing Pyramids with their apex at the Cube's center and their bases on the faces of the Cube. Note that these pyramids are different than the pyramid that perpetuates described in the last section.

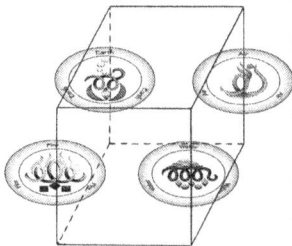

The four vertical edges of the Cube are connected to the elements at the four corners of the Pyramid. This effectively reproduces the Elemental Energies in the center of each vertical edge of the Cube. The six apexes converge at the Cube's center. These diagonal energies provide a flow and connection between the faces and the center of the Cube. This connection provides the 'voice' of the Cube which allows an expression of the energy the Cube is working with. That expression is what is brought into an etheric form, that, in turn, manifests physically.

Formation & the Foundation Energies
NORTH

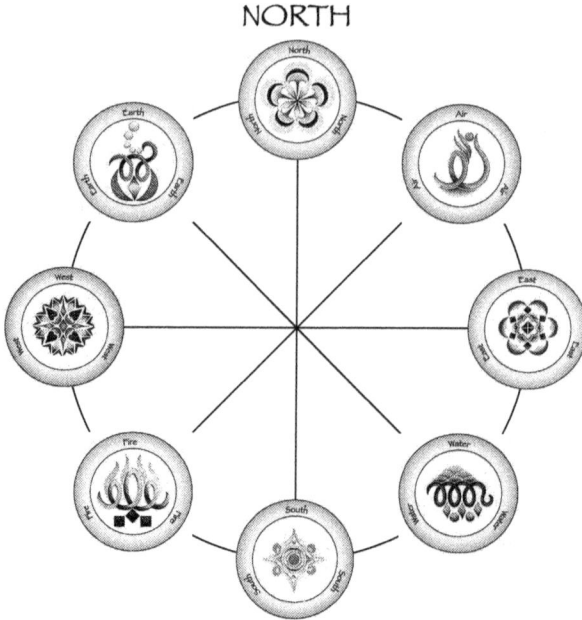

The Foundation Energies provide three sets of ingredients necessary for manifestation to occur; the ingredients for manifestation, (the elements) the perception needed for manifestation, (the directions) and the movement needed to bring together everything needed for manifestation (the winds.)

These twelve energies are always present even if they are not purposely placed or recognized. Every time you have the simplest thought, or build the most complex project the Foundation Energies are present and at work.

The twelve energies occur naturally in the placement shown in the diagram. The directions lined up according to their cardinal directions with the Earth in the North West, the Fire in the South West, the Water in the South East and the Air in the North East. Different arrangements are possible but the diagram shows the most productive and balanced arrangement.

The Foundation Energies are anchored in every sacred site in the four corners of the Pyramid. Their energies feed the site and the site's need to manifest energies that express the identity of the site.

The Four Elements

The elements provide the ingredients for manifestation.

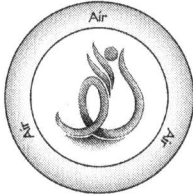

Air creates a Space that allows the manifestation to occur.

Fire creates the movement to bring everything needed to enter the Space created by air.

Water takes the movement and condenses it into something that can be shaped.

Earth takes what can be shaped and solidifies it.

The Four Directions

The directions give perspective to any form of interaction. Without these four perspectives it would be impossible to interpret any form of interaction.

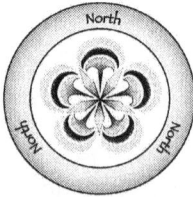

The North represents wisdom and gives an overview of what needs to be manifested.

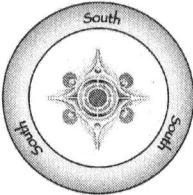

South represents innocence and gives you the details of everything and anything that is needed in order to manifest.

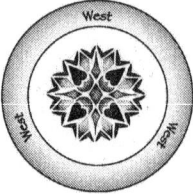

West represents instigation and gets you up and moving along the steps of creation.

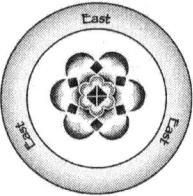

East represents solidity and allows you to see and use the final stable form.

Energy of Sacred Sites

The Four Winds

Additionally, the winds provide the force needed to bring everything into manifestation.

The North wind brings assimilation of all the factors needed to accomplish the goal.

The South wind brings a stable innocence that provides focus and conciseness.

The West wind brings a stimulating movement that energizes the entire process.

The East wind brings an awakening that allows the result to be recognized.

The basis for the above information comes from "Creation It's Laws and You" by June K. Burke.

Placement

Element Lines
Two general arrangements are possible:

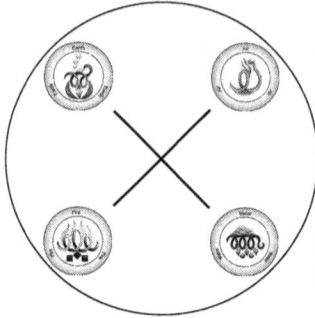

The first alignment is preferred, and is the one found in all sacred site's. It puts earth-water and fire-air across from each other. This arrangement creates a balance between the energies. It also draws the focus into the center of the elements.

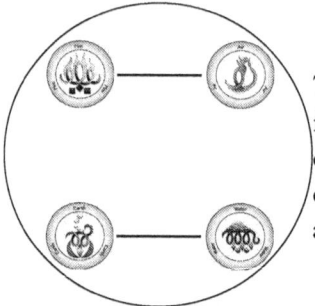

The other alignment puts earth-fire and air-water parallel to each other. This arrangement creates a defocused energy that pushes focus away from the center.

Directional Lines

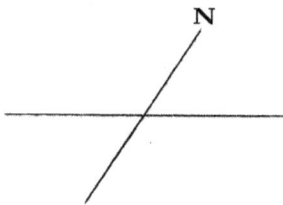

The Directional Lines reach out from the center of the site in true North - South and East - West alignment. They provide the fundamental energies for the expression of the sacred site. The alignment of these Directional Lines also provides a framework for positioning all other energies of the site.

Identity

The Petal Pattern

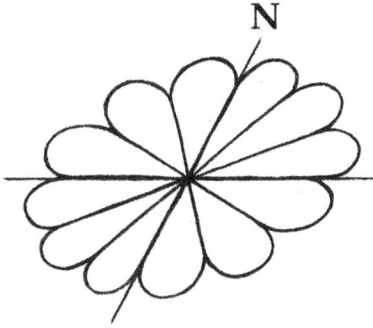

A Petal Pattern is formed the instant a need for interaction occurs. For a sacred site this happens either at the moment of dedication or upon its first use. For a human it is the instant of the first breath at birth. The purpose of the Petal Pattern is to provide an etheric interaction that bridges the physical and spiritual worlds.

Each of us has a permanent Petal Pattern that moves with us wherever we go. Our individual pattern grows in strength whenever we express ourselves. For example when we interact with another person, give a public talk, meditate, etc. Every time we express our identity our pattern expands. In addition, every physical object, such as a chair, a piece of jewelry, a temple, etc. has a Petal Pattern that gives it identity.

The Universal identity of a sacred site can be identified through meditation. In fact, the Petal Pattern is what supplies the energy of psychometry. It is what we psychically tune into when we want to learn more about the spiritual aspect of an object.

Through the Petal Pattern, the sacred site has an ability to provide up-to-date energy as our need or the needs of the Universe change. As Universal needs change, the sacred site is notified. And conversely, as the sacred site changes the Universe is notified. The Petal Pattern maintains a oneness between humanity's needs, Earth's needs and Universal needs. It keeps the Spiral of humanity within the Earth within the Universe in sync.

The Petal Pattern retains the intent of the sacred site much like your natal astrological chart represents the energies you were born with. In your natal chart, for example, all the energies you need for growth are present in your Petal Pattern and available for your free will use. The same is true in the Petal Pattern that is connected to a sacred site. Everything is there to allow the Space to grow and move with and within the Universe.

The Petal Energies

The Petal Energies form a pattern that is divided up into a number of pie shaped segments with rounded edges. These segments are, in reality, a continuum of energy that has no finite number of divisions. However, they can be subdivided into general categories that help describe their properties.

The primary division is the four quadrants bounded by the North - South and East - West Directional Lines.

Each petal contains a receptacle that holds part of the site's identity. This could be thought of as the site's personality without the ego need to be competitive. In other words, the petals hold the pure identity as it was dedicated at the time the physical site was constructed.

The petals coupled with other etheric site structures provide an ability to interact with the Universe or whoever uses the site.

Energy of Sacred Sites

The Four Quadrants

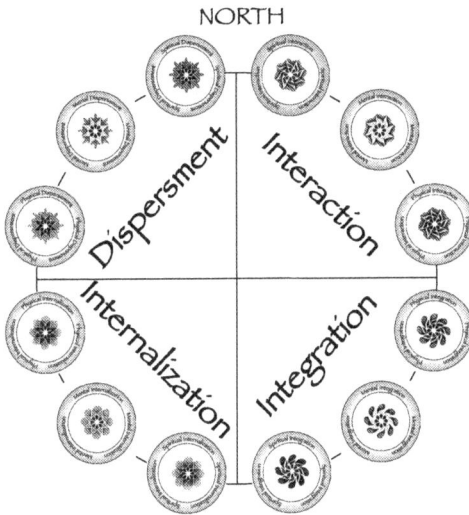

NORTH

Each Petal Pattern is divided into four quadrants along East - West and North - South lines. The quadrants give a general yet unique meaning to the petals. Each quadrant is further divided into three petals, and each petal is divided into seven energies.

The Four Quadrants represent:

1. The energies of Internalization. This South - West quadrant is an inward looking perspective. The relationship between appearance, values and immediate environment can be seen. From a personal perspective, it is how you look at yourself.

2. The energies of Integration. This South - East quadrant brings separate things together in a compatible way. The way things fit together can be seen. From a personal perspective, it is how you feel and think about yourself.

3. The energies of Interaction. This North - East quadrant allows a mixing of energies such that all the components are connected in a way that is useful. Communication is possible. From a personal perspective, it is how you communicate with yourself.

4. The energies of Dispersement. This North - West quadrant breaks up energies in a way that allows new energies to be born. Growth is possible. From a personal perspective, it is how you use your energy in the outside world.

The Three Petals

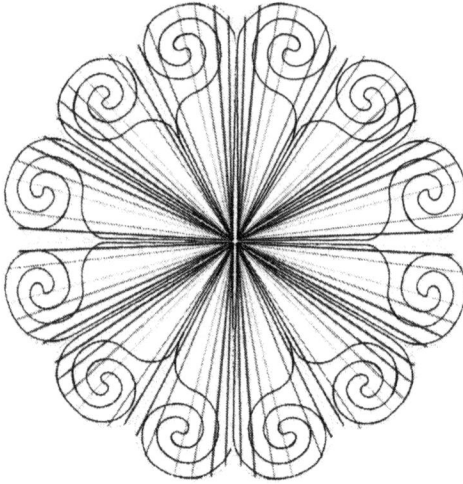

Each quadrant is divided into three sectors or petals. Each petal, in turn, represents physical, mental and spiritual consciousness. The spiritual petal of one quadrant flows into a spiritual petal of the next quadrant. Similarly, the physical petal of one quadrant flows into the physical petal of the next quadrant. The mental petal is always in the middle of the quadrant.

The 7x7x7 Energies

Each petal is then divided into seven energies which flow into the next in a seamless way. Each of the seven energies are subsequently divided into seven energies and so on. These seven divisions are similar to the energies of the chakras, represented as earth, water, fire, air, space, mind and Universe. The Universal energy of one petal flows into the Universal energy of the next petal.

The energy of each petal starts at its source, the center of the Petal Pattern, and reaches out through the three levels of physical, mental and spiritual consciousness as represented by the Spiral.

Each petal has within it the seven levels of consciousness. So the seven levels of the Spiral of spirit, mind and body moves through the four quadrants of internalization, integration, interaction and dispersement, at three levels of physical, mental and spiritual, that are in turn divided into seven levels of consciousness. This gives 7x3x4x3x7 = 1764 separate interaction points. Whew! This means that there are ample opportunities for the energies to reach you at the proper level of consciousness.

The Petal Pattern bears a strong resemblance to the system of houses in astrology.

The 12 Receptacle Energies

The end of each petal contains a receptacle that holds energy which serves two purposes. The first purpose is to communicate with all aspects of its identity as defined by its birth or its dedication. The second purpose is to hold the state of whatever is undergoing interaction from moment to moment. It is a holding area that keeps the purpose of the interaction alive until a new understanding is achieved. The energy of each petal loops around the receptacle and mixes its contents with the other parts of the complex.

In part V, the chapter on Receptacle Energies gives a detailed description of each petal energy, starting in the petal just South of West and going counter-clockwise. The descriptions are written from the site's point of view. Remember that everything that needs a Universal connection is alive, has an unique identity and can be related to as a living being. Perhaps the descriptions can be related to more easily if you remember that you are a sacred site.

Evolution

The Wisdom Circle

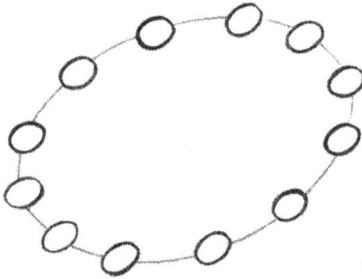

Clarity is maintained through an etheric group of energies that are named the Wisdom Circle. Basically, the Wisdom Circle is there to provide a wise base to the use of the site. In addition, the site's purity needs to be perpetuated over the life of the site, and this is also accomplished by the Wisdom Circle. If it wasn't for the Wisdom Circle, the energy of the site would quickly degrade the purity of its original purpose.

When a sacred site is created it is given a purpose. The purpose may be stated in detail by the architect, or by the intent of the creator, or verbalized in its dedication ceremony. Or, its purpose may be implied through its use. Either way, the site receives a purpose.

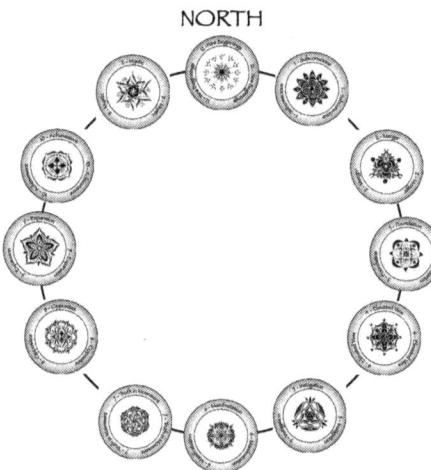

NORTH

It is the job of the Wisdom Circle to provide clarity for that purpose. In other words, the Wisdom Circle is the Universe's response to the site's purpose. The Wisdom Circle is made up of twelve unique energies that are precisely arranged according to true North - South and East - West alignments. The twelve energies represent twelve different arenas that allow higher level spiritual interaction to be clarified in the physical world.

Energy of Sacred Sites

The twelve stations of the Wisdom Circle represent New Beginnings, Subconscious, Merger, Foundation, Elevated View, Instigation, Manifestation, Truth in Movement, Opposite's, Expansion, Achievement and the Mystic.

These are pure energies and not their physical representation. For instance, the mystic represents the energy that is mystical, not the person who is the mystic, or for that matter, who uses the mystic energy. Each of the twelve energies represents a unique aspect of pure Universal consciousness.

The Wisdom Circle creates clarity via movement of Universal energy, through its segments, in a manner that allows the energy to be physically or emotionally felt. The Wisdom Circle modulates Universal energy in a way that identifies the purpose of the sacred site. Continual flow of energy keeps the purpose pure - at least without considerable human intervention.

Universal Wisdom

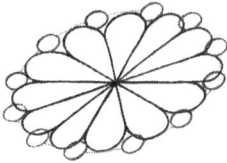

The Wisdom Circle and the Petal Pattern provide a source of Universal wisdom in interactive form. That source energy can be tapped in a way that allows intellectual understanding through the identity of the site. The understanding occurs independently of the pre-conceived notion humanity chooses, and always reflects the sacred site's identity. In other words, the structures present wisdom. It is humanity's free will choice as to its use.

These structures become an active filter between the spiritual energy that found purpose at the time the sacred site was created, and the use humanity makes of the site. This means the structures help keep the sacred site from corruption beyond its dedicated purpose. Of course, the site's purpose can be changed. However, the structures keep this change from becoming an instantaneous or chaotic transformation driven by the whim of random participants. This guarantees that the changes will occur over an appropriate period of time and in an orderly and gentle manner.

Memory

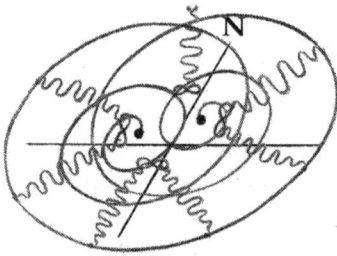

The site maintains a memory through a number of structures that include, Dispersed and Siren Structures, that broadcast the identity of the site much like the song of a whale. There are involuted Spirals that intertwine and collect and mix energies. And there are a pair of key site's that maintain a firm grip on the site's identity.

Dispersed Structure

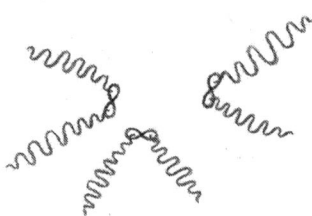

The Dispersed Structure is made up of three pairs of Laniscates that broadcast their particular energy to corresponding pairs of dispersed points. The three pairs relate to magnetic, electrical and physical energies. Each pare represents polarities of their related energies. Through their vibration, these pairs of energies produce a melody of sound that maintains balance with the changing Universal energies. The Laniscates create an etheric music that becomes more earthy at the extremities of the structure. The line of energy that connects the Laniscates with the corresponding extremity rises and falls in volume and rhythm so the melody has purpose.

The Siren Structure

A seventh dispersed site has the ability to create a symphony of sound that carries with it the musical essence of the site. The symphony is composed of the melodies of the Dispersed Structures and theme of the key structure.

The Siren Structure not only calls the Universal or spiritual energies, it also calls us humans to the site through intuition. With careful meditation the site's symphony can be actually heard.

Energy of Sacred Sites

Involuted Spiral

The Involuted Spiral circulates the information carried in the key structures and distributes them to the Dispersed and Siren Structures. This allows the primary energy of the site to be maintained.

Key Structure

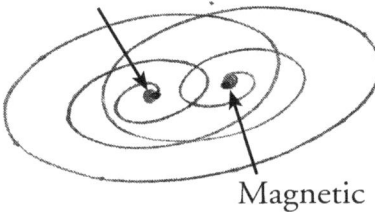

The Key Structures maintain a consistent identity, even though the Universe and Earth change, they provide the underlying theme for the changing melodies of the Dispersed Structures. The theme is the essence of the sacred site's identity and purpose.

One key represents the electrical, or fire nature of the identity while the other key represents the magnetic, or water nature. These electrical and magnetic keys have the capability to contain everything that is needed for the site to retain its identity over millenniums of time.

Universal Connection

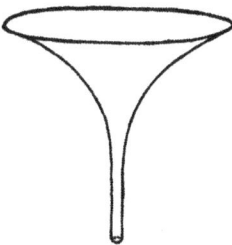

Extending upward, from the center of the site, is a communication line that connects the sacred site with the Universe. This line also extends downward into the Earth such that an Earth - Universe connection is established. The vertical connection anchors the higher, spiritual perspective of the Universe with a more practical, earthy need. This connection and interaction is analogous to the neuron - synapse connection within the brain.

We have found that meditating while sitting on this spot gives a greater clarity and more succinct interaction. This is because meditating here allows you to be in two places at once, the practical Earth and the wise Universe. It takes a bit of getting used to, but, once achieved, there is a clear flow of interaction that presents itself in a way that makes sense and is useful.

Universal Access

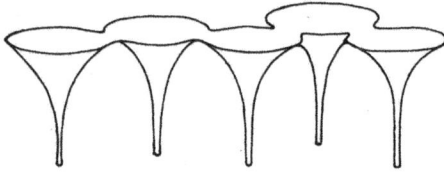

Universal connections are connected to other Universal connections in a way that assures that everything in the Universe is connected.

Access to, and interaction with the Universe (bridging between Earth and Universe) happens at the memory structure and its Universal Connection that is centered on a crossing of North - South and East - West energies. Also located at that directional crossing is the Four Pole Magnet. This combination of energies produces a Pulse that reaches down into the Earth and up into the Universe. This movement serves to connect the whole structure to the Universe. It provides a two way link between the clarified and stabilized sacred site and the Universe.

This structure is associated with sacred site's and all living things. Or, perhaps more accurately, it is in everything that needs to touch the Universe.

Energy Flow

Flow Through the Site

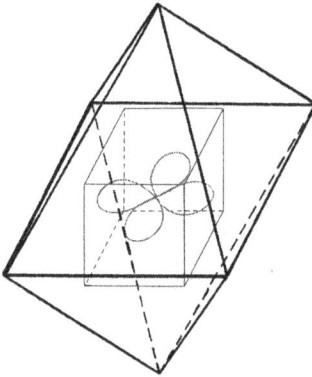

Energy movement is accomplished through the etheric components we call the Pyramid, the Double Laniscate, the Cube of Space and the Foundation Energies. The Pyramid anchors and perpetually recirculates the energies. The Cube of Space provides the arena that allows manifestation to come into form. The Double Laniscate provides the mechanism that manifests the energies. The Foundation Energies provide the ingredients for manifestation to occur. The energies interact with each other through connecting Spirals.

Connecting Spirals

Each end of the flow circulates in a Spiraling manner that connects the energy at one end with energy at the other end. The flow is kept in motion by a vortex of energy approximately half way between the ends of the flow.

The flow turns at each end, becomes an ever decreasing loop of a Spiral, until the Spiral becomes a point of energy. The Spiral then reverses upon itself and expands back out into a line that returns to the Spiral at the other end.

Active and Receptive Energy Flow

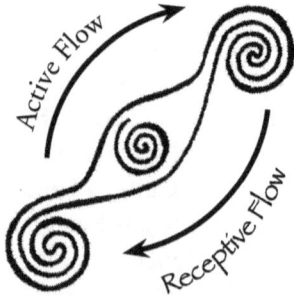

All the energy lines in a site are connected in a way that allows flow between end points in the line. The result is two lines of energy, one active and the other receptive, flowing in different directions.

The Delivery of Elemental Energies

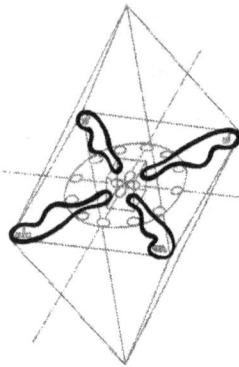

Elemental Energies flow from the corners of the Pyramids to the edges of the Cube of Space. This moves the ingredients for manifestation into an arena that allows manifestation. The steps of manifestation move within the arena of the Cube of Space and physically manifest the purpose of the sacred site. The double Laniscate absorbs the energy of the Wisdom Circle, then circulates and manifests whatever the Wisdom Circle has clarified. The North - South Laniscate takes the overview perspective into the details. The West - East Laniscate takes the creative work into its final form. The Double Laniscate is entirely contained within the Cube of space. Its crossing point resides at the exact center of the Cube.

There is an energy flow between the Wisdom Circle and the Four pole magnet. This connects each wisdom energy with the cross point of the double Laniscate, however, only one connection is shown. This pattern is identical to the connection for all other components of a sacred site.

Energy of Sacred Sites

How the Pulse Works

The Pulse of the sacred site is an important element because it pumps the life force through the site. Through the contraction, expansion and twisting of the Four Pole Magnet, the energy Spirals out, then back forming a Pulse of energy. As the Spiral returns upon itself, a never ending movement of energy in the form of concentric circles moves out. These circles of energy touch and return continuously sensing and receiving what is outside of the site.

The Pyramid and Four Pole Magnet work together to create and perpetuate the action of the Pulse.

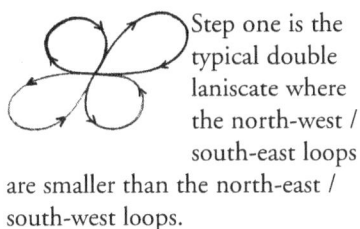

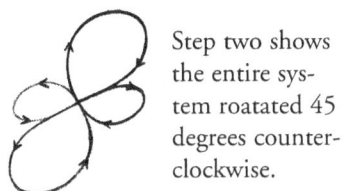

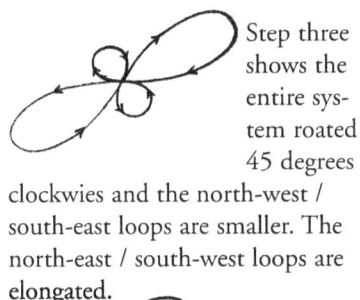

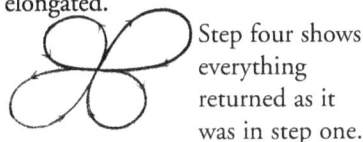

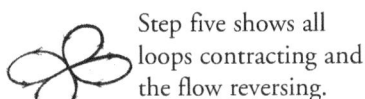

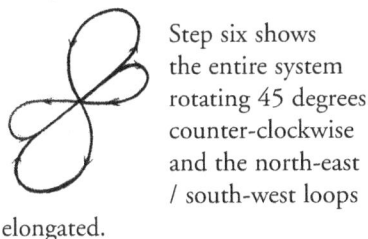

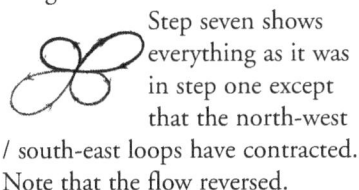

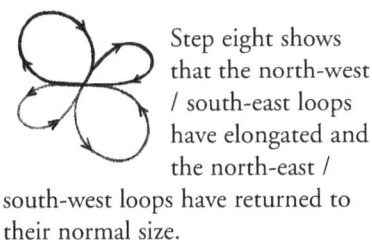

Step one is the typical double laniscate where the north-west / south-east loops are smaller than the north-east / south-west loops.

Step two shows the entire system roatated 45 degrees counter-clockwise.

Step three shows the entire system roated 45 degrees clockwies and the north-west / south-east loops are smaller. The north-east / south-west loops are elongated.

Step four shows everything returned as it was in step one.

Step five shows all loops contracting and the flow reversing.

Step six shows the entire system rotating 45 degrees counter-clockwise and the north-east / south-west loops elongated.

Step seven shows everything as it was in step one except that the north-west / south-east loops have contracted. Note that the flow reversed.

Step eight shows that the north-west / south-east loops have elongated and the north-east / south-west loops have returned to their normal size.

The Energy Flow in the Petal Pattern

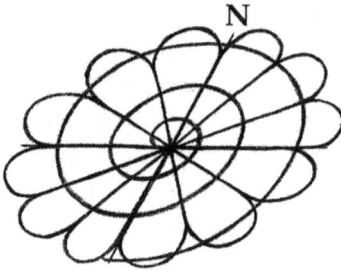

In order to understand how the energy flow occurs in a Petal Pattern, we need to look at the three components of the Petal Pattern. At first glance this seems a bit complex. However, each part has a definite function and expression of Universal consciousness. The three components are:

1. A crossing of North - South and East - West Directional Lines that fix its position and give it permanence while providing Universal perspective.

2. A set of petal-like divisions that provide the storehouse for the levels of consciousness needed for complete interaction.

3. A pulsing Spiral that provides interaction via movement of energy and thought.

If you sit at the center of a Petal Pattern and pose a question, the following actions occur:

1. The question moves outward along the Spiral, passing through the petals. This provides an expression at every level of consciousness.

2. The answer moves inward along the Spiral and passes through the petals. This provides an answer or clarity towards an answer at every level of consciousness. The Directional Lines provide the perspective.

This energy flow occurs every time we express ourselves with a question or statement. In other words, the Universe is involved with our every thought or action. The hard part for humanity is to listen to what the Universe has to say. It is what the Universe says, that shows our growth path.

Communication

Each sacred site needs a support system in order to interface with the physical world. The site needs ears in order to prepare for changes and a voice that announces its presence.

We humans understand and sense this support by feeling the site's unique energy. We react to needs. For example, by adding a room onto our house or by taking a vacation. The site's needs come from a Universal creative source and react to environmental or Earth changes in a way that perpetuates the site's energy in keeping with the Universal changes.

Whenever there is a significant Universal change about to happen, like at the cusp of a new age or when Earth changes are necessary, the site disperses its energies for safe keeping. This dispersal is accomplished through etheric structures that allow the old site's energy to be upgraded to a new Universal energy.

We have all experienced the inner personal adjustments that have been necessary for us as the higher energies of the aquarian age began to be felt. The sacred site's need to make a similar adjustment and the support system accomplishes that through what we call dispersed and key structures.

Communication happens through Ley Lines, a five pointed star, link site's and the site's guardians.

Sacred Site or Ley Lines

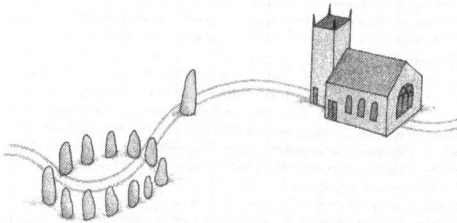

There are often connections between physical sacred site's that are commonly called Ley Lines. We have chosen to call these lines Sacred Site Lines to differentiate them from other energy lines and fields that we will get into later in this book.

These Sacred Site Lines serve to connect physical site's that have a similar energy. The lines have a double flow that depicts a male - female or active - receptive energy. In fact these lines are identical to the Connecting Spiral that is described in the chapter on Energy Flow. In addition, many of these lines have been written about in great detail so we won't cover them in detail here. We can however, recommend the book by Miller and Broadhurst, "The Sun and the Serpent."

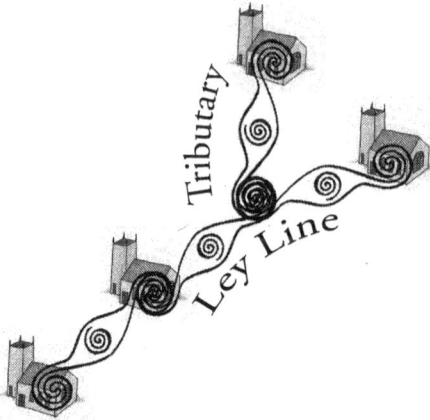

The chapter on Energy Flow describes in more detail how sacred site's are configured and operate. Also other lines, such as song lines are similar to the flow of energy between sacred site's. Multiple similar site's are connected via segments where each segment is identical to the flow of energy within the site. In addition, a branch of the line may be formed to continue in another direction. Whenever a line stops and another begins there is a reversal in the active / receptive energy flow.

The distance between endpoints may be significant. Some lines have been measured in excess of 25 miles. In fact some Ley Lines seem to be many hundreds of miles long. However closer inspection via dowsing reveals the lines are actually made up of many smaller lines connected together as shown in the diagram.

Energy of Sacred Sites

Link Sites

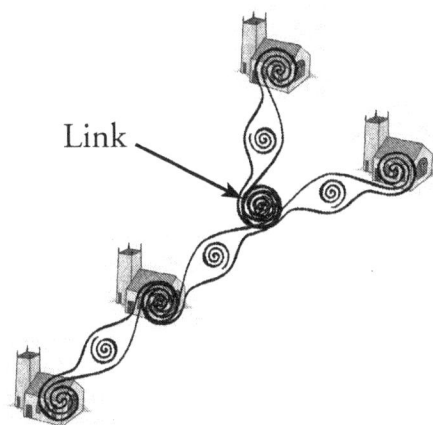

Link

Many sacred sites are interconnected via energy lines. These lines are different than the lines that connect sacred sites in order to propagate a particular energy.

Spaces are linked when they have a common Universal purpose or expression, independently of the purpose humanity has assigned to them. As Universal needs expand and contract, the Space can be linked or delinked via Link Sites. The linking (or delinking) is automatic whenever the similarities (or differences) in vibration between two sited becomes similar (or too great.) Or, in other words, the identity of the two site's converges or diverges.

Each Link Site connects with three, or on rare occasions more, sacred sites and provides a flow of energy that supports the space. Some sacred sites are directly linked to another sacred site without passing through a Link Site.

Support System and Maintenance

Star Patterns

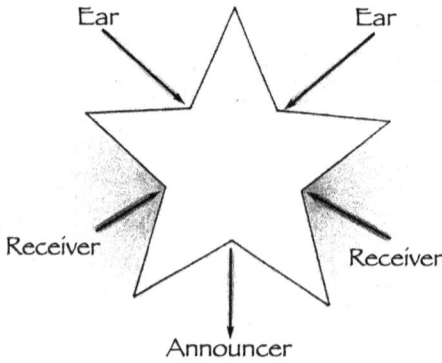

Star patterns are often, but not always associated with a large, natural sacred site, such as a mystical grove or rock formation. The five pointed star pattern provides the eyes and ears of the Earth that give nature sensory interaction between the Earth and the Universe.

Stars connect with a sacred site via an energy line between the star and the site's etheric Pyramid. This energy line announces the stars sensory findings to the sacred site. The Pyramid recirculates the energy to the Complex of Interaction to then to the Universe.

Diamond Areas

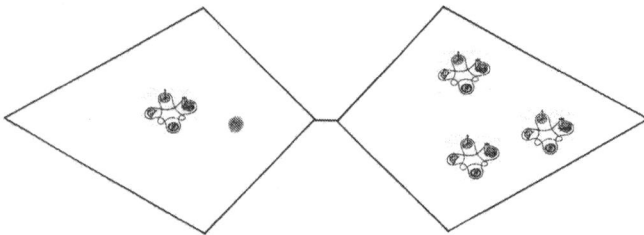

Often large areas have a significant need to have their purpose guarded from corruption. These areas may have important physical sacred sites or contain more naturally occurring site's that support nature. The areas are diamond shaped and usually occur in connected pairs and are usually aligned North - South.

Energy of Sacred Sites

Guardians

Guardians are etheric beings which reside at a spot within the Guardian Area and, with care and respect, can be contacted. These guardians are different from the guardians associated with every individual sacred site.

Every sacred site has an etheric, or spirit guardian that keeps watch over the site. If there are a number of similar site's in the same geographic diamond shaped area, a single guardian may watch over them all. The Guardian's job is to act as an early warning for the site's use or abuse. The Guardian can interact with visitors, including spirit, human or animal.

We have found it quite easy to interact with the site's guardian in order to gain more knowledge about the site's purpose and history. Interaction with the Guardian is described in the chapter on "Using the Sacred Site." There is great respect shown for the site Guardians. Their job can last for eons of time and their dedication is unrivaled.

Part II
The Connection With The Earth

Outward and Inward Funnels

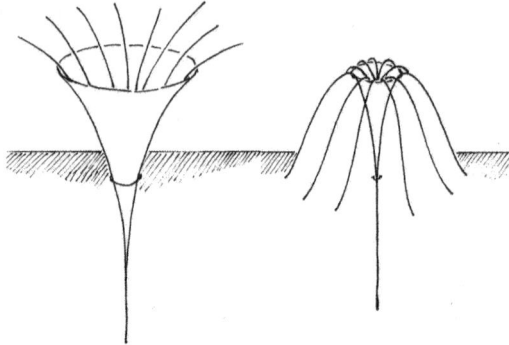

Outward Funnel   Inward Funnel

Funnels are large umbrella like etheric formations that move energy in a way that helps in the Earth's process of physical renewal.

The Outward Funnel moves energy up from the depths of the Earth and distributes it in an area of about a thirty mile radius. The Inward Funnel moves energy from the Earths surface back into the depths of the Earth for safekeeping until time to re-project them.

There are a small number of funnels distributed through the world and they wax and wane as a need exists.

Connection with Earth

The Earth as an Interconnected System

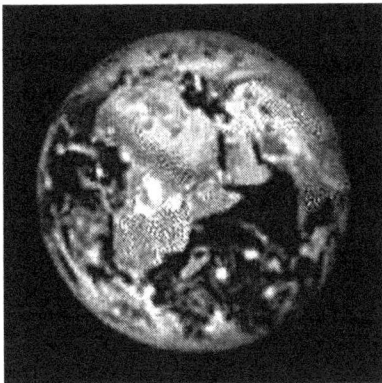

We have found lots of interesting information about the energies that maintain a structure that literally holds the Earth together. There are Grid Lines that form a fixed pattern providing a glue that literally keeps the Earth together. And there are ley fields that form a cover of energy that moves as the need for shifts occur. These energies are part of a two way link between the Earth and the Universe that are a part of the Complex of Interaction described in a previous chapter. We have mapped and continue to verify these Grid Lines and ley fields in Europe and the U.S.

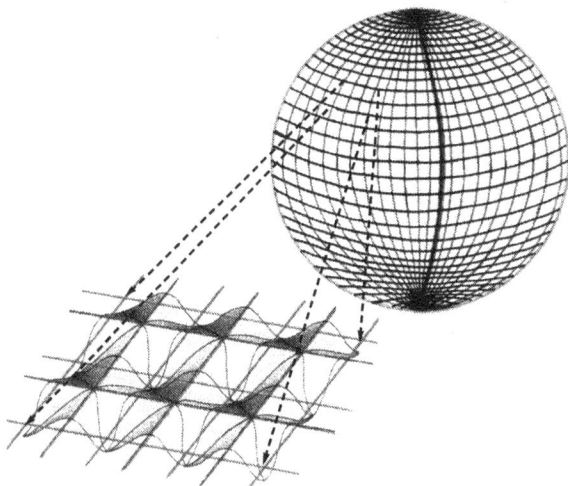

Basically, what we have found is that the Earth has the same energy patterns surrounding it that all sentient beings have. There is no difference between the Earth and its energy structures and the energy patterns that surround each of us. The Earth has a connection to the Universe as do we. This chapter introduces Grid Lines and ley fields that form part of the infrastructure, that are part of the Complex of Interaction and provide the glue that holds the Earth together.

The grid and ley energies are strong, but difficult to detect because of their unique energies. In order to locate them, work at the three levels of physical, mental and spiritual consciousness is needed. This means a lot of dowsing, meditation, study and physical work.

When any energy system is found, its purpose needs to be understood. Otherwise, what use does it have? How can it grow corn? To answer that, we need to look at the energies of Grid Lines and ley fields in more detail.

Grid Lines

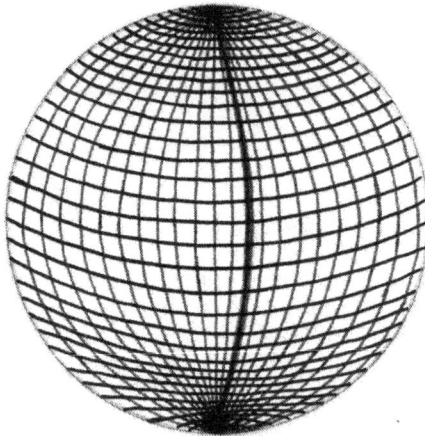

There are 84 North/South latitudinal Grid Lines that encircle the Earth. The Grid Lines are magnetic in nature and appear in a fixed pattern. There is another set of East/West Grid Lines that circle the Earth in an longitudinal direction. There are 184 loops spaced such that each loop forms squares with the N - S lines. This crossing of lines forms a predictable grid pattern that covers the Earth. If the Earth is viewed from one of its poles, the N - S lines appear as a Petal Pattern moving out from its center. The width of each individual Grid Line is about two kilometers.

The grid follows energies identical to the Petal Pattern described in the chapter on the Petal Pattern. This means that the Earth itself is a giant sacred site who's structure repeats itself down to the tiniest living thing. In addition, the Grid Lines interact in partnership with other Earth energies. The interaction provides the basis for maintaining balance through communication with the Universe and every thing that is part of the Earth.

Connection with Earth

The grid and ley energies are reproduced as part of the human aura. The grid - ley interaction gives movement to the aura as well as help in the adjustments necessary for balance to occur. The aura formed by the grid and ley energies can be found in every sentient being, or anything that interacts with the Universe.

Ley Fields

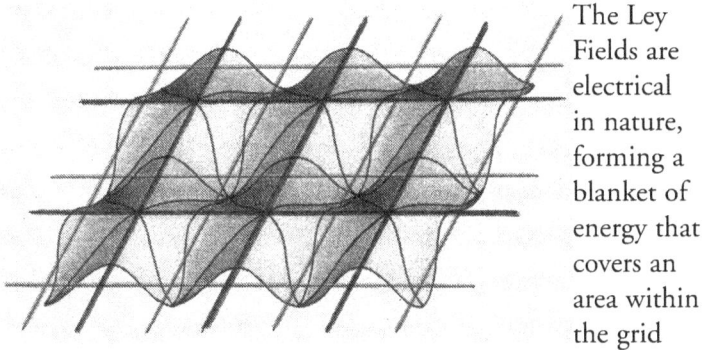

The Ley Fields are electrical in nature, forming a blanket of energy that covers an area within the grid squares.

Ley Fields are in constant choreographed movement. The choreography stems from a need for the Earth to evolve as the Universe evolves. If the Earth needs to physically change in order to remain balanced, the Ley Fields warp. The warping creates a tension that creates a physical reaction. The reaction may be in the form of whatever Earth or atmospheric movement necessary in order to relieve the tension.

Ley Fields divide a grid square into four quadrants, representing the four elements. These four elemental quadrants form what we call a Four Pole Magnet. The end points of earth and water form two poles and the air fire ends form another set of poles.

Flow Lines

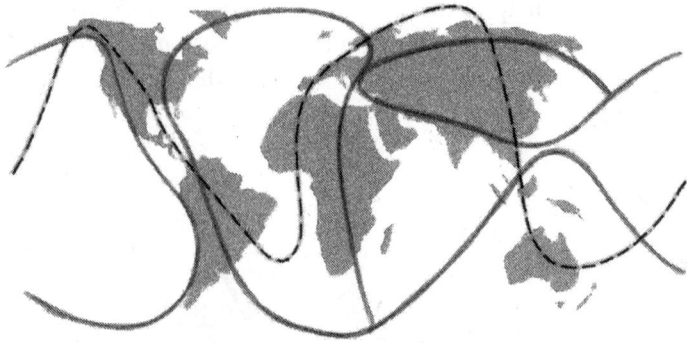

There are two major lines that depict the flow, or movement of energy around and through the Earth. One line contains the flow of atmospheric energy (the dotted line) and the other is the flow of more physical Earth energy.

The Earth line is more internal to the Earth's surface while the atmosphere line is more external to the Earth's surface. The lines can be dowsed and are about 160 miles wide.

The lines do not indicate the precise area where Earth or atmospheric activity will occur. They do, however, show the probable arena where most activity does occur.

Connection with Earth

Changes in the Earth

We all know, through experience, that there is an escalation of energies during the Solstices and Equinoxes. There are two reasons for this escalation. Today we are at the beginning of the Aquarian Age, a 2,600 year period of time which brings changes to the consciousness of the Universe, Earth and humanity.

We are also at the beginning of a 3,000 year Round that marks a time of physical adjustment necessary for humanity to be sustained on the Earth. The Age change provides a mechanism for our consciousness to Spiral upward in our Universal evolution. The Round provides a mechanism for the Earth to bring physical rest to areas that have been over active, and to allow unused physical areas to become productive. In short, we are now experiencing a double whammy of change that is ushering in a greater sense of brotherhood to a physically changing Earth.

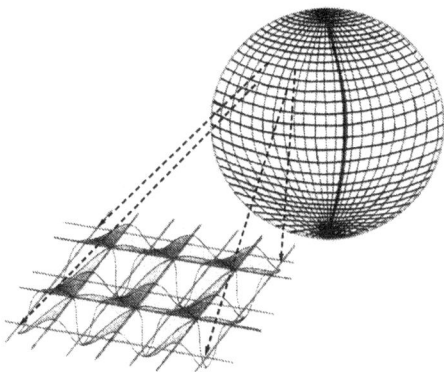

Happily, the grid and ley structures we described keep the whole process from getting out of wack and they encourage a strong partnership with the Universe. Interaction of the grid and ley energies keeps the Earth balanced. The need for a new balance comes from the escalation of Universal energies, which in turn creates a need for changes in humanity's consciousness and environment. As might be expected, the need for new balance is alive and well today as we experience the cusp of the new millennium.

For example: During a Round change, the Universal energy escalates and imparts the shift on the Earth. The lines respond and warp as necessary in order to accommodate the shift. The degree of change is determined by need but contained by the Grid Lines. In this case, determination of "need" results from environmental conditions, and by the thinking patterns and actions of the people who populate the area. As change occurs, the Universe is signaled and it responds. Then the lines settle down, becoming a new point of balance. Movement and communication continue until harmony is achieved.

This means that as the Universe changes, the Earth, with humanity as its passengers, follows. Negative attitudes and/or environmental needs influence the system of grid and ley energies. In other words, the lines form a unique bio-feedback system that creates and maintains Universal balance. If the "suggested" changes are ignored, the Universe responds by pushing harder. The whole process helps humanity accept the new energies in a manner that constructively expands awareness.

Because of the escalation in Universal energy we find that our values are changing. Our actions, driven by new values, make a tremendous difference. More than ever before our healing meditations, prayers and actions influence the Earth. By living, not resisting, our new values, we release tension and help create harmonious changes in the Earth. This creates a never ending and always moving partnership between humanity and the Universe. We are part of the loop!

The field warps or stretches into polarities of active and quiet areas. If the ratio of active - quiet areas changes significantly, tension is created between the ley - grid energies. Warping can be created by energy changes or by people's thinking patterns. This warping signals a need for physical realignment, and/or, the need for a change in humanities consciousness.

All this means that a strong warping in ley fields is an early warning system indicating areas that are in need of change. However, some changes are inevitable because the Earth needs to rest or awaken. So, healing the Earth really means helping the ley fields facilitate harmonious Earth changes. It is important to work with the lines such that negative thought doesn't amplify the need for change. The changes are for our benefit. Without them our evolution would stagnate.

Connection with Earth

Strength

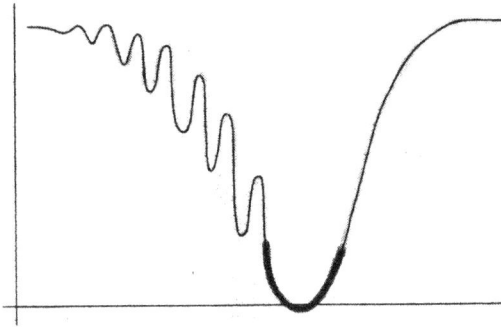

Strength of the grid - ley system can be measured through dowsing. We have measured the grid/ ley strength on trips throughout the United States and Europe and have found three interesting things:

First, the strength can decrease from 100% to close to 0% over a 54 month period.

Second, during this decreasing period, the strength will bounce up six or seven times. Each bounce is less that the previous strength, and follows a decreasing pattern until minimum strength is found.

Third, many of the bounces are accompanied by some strong Earth reaction, such as earthquakes or flooding. The Earths reaction intensifies as the strength falls below 20%.

The Bottom Line

The interaction of grid and ley energies creates tension between their magnetic and electrical properties. Continued strong electrical tension will give way to earth and fire shifts. Continued strong magnetic tension gives way to water and air movement. Taken to extremes the ley - grid energies are indications of earthquakes, volcanic activity, floods and storms. Yes Mabel, Earth changes can be predicted! Remember however, Earth changes renew the Earth to support the evolutionary process of humanity.

Ley - grid interaction guarantees that the Earth can regain balance, meaning it can remain happily habitable by us humans, even if we have abused it. It is our consciousness and acceptance of the changes that, in part, determine the need for Earth change.

Earth changes are beneficial because they help adjust the Earth's and humanity's energy to match Universal evolution. The changes also renew the Earth so we can continue to live productively. When we are "in tune" with Universal changes, the Earth changes are softened. Because of the shift in Universal energies, this is a good time for Earth healing through prayer, meditation and ritual. This is also a time for us to fine tune our thoughts and actions. We can powerfully influence what happens at this beginning of a new age and Round. We are partners with the Earth and the Universe, linked by the grid and ley networks, and by the presence of similar patterns within ourselves.

Part III Practicality

If this section may seem a bit sketchy, realize that everyone is unique and will have a unique way to use the information. The reader is encouraged to take this basic information and mold it into a methodology that works best for them.

So, How Does It Grow Corn?

Now, take a deep breath; here is the whole concept in one sentence. The sacred site is identified by humanity's purpose which is connected to the Universe, given identity, has the ability to interact by the Petal Pattern, purified by the Wisdom Circle and anchored by the Pyramid.

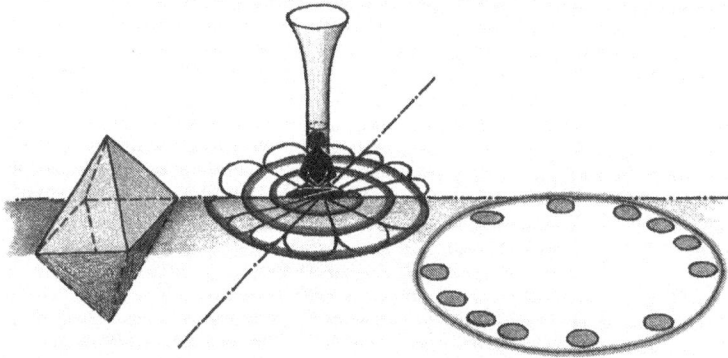

In order to open communication with the Universe all you need to do is to go to, or create, a sacred site, then find the Petal Pattern that is linked to the site. It's guaranteed to be there. Then sit at the center of the complex and allow yourself to become part of the link through merging and pulsing with all the components. Or, if you wish, just meditate! When you meditate you become a sacred site and the Universe will reach out and automatically create all the components in close proximity to you. You will be connected to pure clarity with a perpetuating anchor of the energy in a way that is best for you and your spiritual growth. The Petal Pattern in you, as the sacred site, defines the arena for the meditation to function.

You then provide the focus to your meditation.

The nice thing about sacred site's is that you do not need to know anything about their etheric components in order for them to work for you. Their meaning, energies and how they are created is a detail that can be left to the Universe. However, if the details are understood, the site's power and ability to perform its task is increased.

Creation of a Sacred Site

The first component of a sacred site is its physical presence. This can be anything that takes up physical space, even if there is no physical object involved. It can be a person, a house, a meditation room or even the Space in your backyard that is used to meditate.

The simple way to create a sacred site is to state a purpose and then meditate. It really is that simple. The arena that is needed to receive guidance is created at the instant the purpose is stated. The energy expands when the purpose is put to use through meditation. Here meditation is meant to be "listening to the quiet voice within," or, to the Universal creative force. Meditation results in a healing energy or an interactive energy that provides guidance. Following the guidance or letting the healing energy work is a matter of free will choice.

This is a good time to go into the details of the process for creating and using a sacred site. These details will help you to understand how to create a more permanent sacred site and one that grows stronger with use. The following describes the steps that help to increase the power of the site. I have a tendency to look at the following information as factual because I have worked with it for so many years. However, it's a good idea to verify it for yourself through dowsing or meditative attunement. Belief goes a long way in the creative process. Faith is important, and faith begins the process of believing. Ultimate truth or belief also requires intellectual understanding because nothing can be taken for granted.

The steps to create a sacred sit:

1 - The preparation of the space.
2 - The dedication of its purpose.
3 - The placing of the energies.

Through motivation the above steps create a physical site or object that allows all the etheric components of a sacred site to form. Let's now look at how to perform the process to create a sacred site in more detail.

Step 1: Preparation of the Space

The first step in the preparation of a site is to create a sacred circle of purification and protection around it. This should always be done around the area that the physical site will occupy. Repeating the sacred circle process each time the site is used will increase its power and usefulness enormously.

Scribing a Circle for Spiritual Work

Scribing means drawing a circle around the Space that is to be used as a sacred site. The following is a simple ritual that has meaning deep in the roots of humanity. We have found that it creates a Space that allows powerful and productive energies to emerge.

When scribing the circle, it is best to walk the area that is to be used, but if that is not possible, you can stand in the center and point to the circle as you are scribing it. The circle can even be scribed mentally if it is best not to be seen.

Always enter and leave the circle from the East. Entering from the East serves to announce to the site that you come in with your present energy and are ready for new perspectives.

1 - Choose a Space that is good for the work that you will be doing.
2 - While scribing a counter-clockwise circle 3 times around the space, say: "I call upon the powers of the Heaven and the

Earth to merge and mix, purifying this space"

When finished say: "Thank you powers of the Heaven and Earth for purifying this space."

3 - While scribing a clockwise circle 3 times around the purified space, say: "I call upon the power of the Creative Force to protect this space."

When finished say: "Thank you power of the Creative Force for protecting this space."

Then say: "So be it!"

To release the Space after your work is finished, enter the circle from the East and with an upward counter-clockwise motion of your hand, say: "I release the energies to their source. Thank you powers for the purification and the protection. So be it!"

The energy of the circle will stay around with use, but it will dissipate when not used. Not releasing the energies is a sign of disrespect. The release will not remove the energies; it only serves to return them to their source for rest. It is best to create and release the circle each time you need it. This keeps the energy fresh and powerful.

Step 2: Dedication of Purpose

This step shows the Universe what the site is going to be used for. Now, you can't fool the Universe. If you declare that the site is going to be used for meditation and you use the site for bingo, the Universe will follow bingo and the energies of meditation will be diminished. When the site is used for the dedicated purpose, far greater power is brought forward.

There are eight Foundation Energies that manifest and give perspective to a sacred site. The elements of earth, water, fire and air are the Universal ingredients that bring into manifestation anything that exists, be it a physical object or a thought. There are also the four directions of North, South, East and West, that give perspective to whatever will be manifested. These eight energies are honored and placed within the sacred circle in order to bring in all the ingredients and perspectives needed to manifest and use the sacred site.

After scribing the sacred circles, use the following process to dedicate the site:

1 - Enter the circle from the East and stand in the middle.

2 - State clearly and concisely what the site's purpose is and then so dedicate it.

3 - Next raise a witness that represents the purpose of the site above your head, then at your forehead and then at your solar plexus as you face each of the four cardinal directions. This honors the directions and brings in the highest perspective needed for whatever work the sacred site will be put to.

The witness may be a piece of paper with the site's purpose written on it, or a physical object or icon that symbolically represents the site's purpose as depicted by the cards supplied with this book. For example, if the site is to be used for study, select a witness such as a notebook, or a piece of paper with the word "study" written on it. Then say with as much purpose and focus as you can muster, the following: "I declare this purified and protected Space to be used for study, and I so dedicate it."

Then face in order North, South, West and East, raising the witness above your head, then at your forehead, and finally at your solar plexus.

Then finally say: "So be it!"

The definitions of the directions stem from their etheric energy. The classical cardinal directions stem from the definitions but have a more dense form. By honoring the directions you allow their perspectives to become active. By holding the witness above your head, at your forehead and at your solar plexus, you bring the perspective to your spirit, your mind and your body.

The basic meaning of the directions are:

North: The overview perspective. (Wisdom)
South: The detail perspective. (Innocence)
West: The active thrust and the creative work. (Instigation)
East: The final form and maintenance of that which has been created. (Foundation)

Step 3: Placing the Elemental Energies

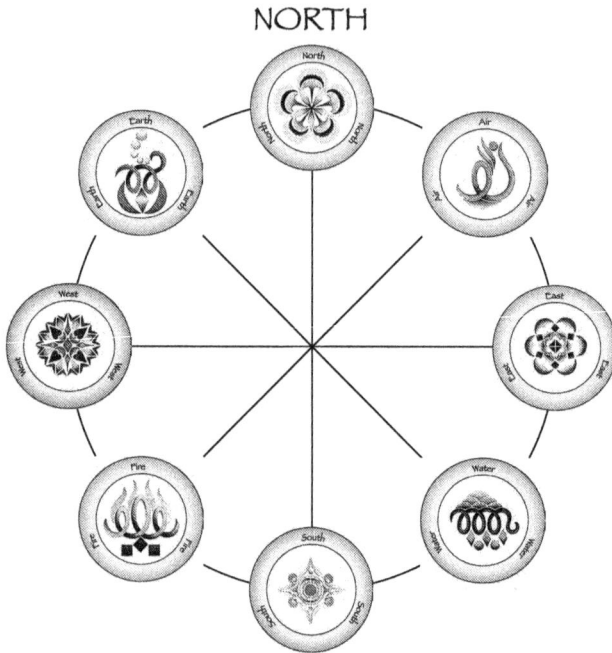

The next step in the creation of a sacred site is to place the energies of manifestation. These energies are called the Elemental Energies. The elements represent the energies of manifestation, and using a ritual to place the Elemental Energies, manifests the site's purpose. At this point some people may accuse us of skirting the twilight zone of physics. Remember, we are describing the metaphysical process of manifestation, and the metaphysical perspective needs to be experienced in order for the physical process to become more real. As you use and understand the elements, manifestation does indeed become easier and occurs more rapidly.

To place the energies of manifestation, move to the position the element will occupy, according to the diagram above, and clearly say: "I place the energy of earth here."

Then deliberately and purposefully place a witness of the earth element on its North - West spot.

Repeat the process for water on its South - East spot, fire on its South - West spot and air on its North - East spot.

The witness can be a stone for earth, a glass of water for water, a candle for fire and a feather or incense for air. Or, if you prefer, the name of the element written on a piece of paper. The cards provided with this book contain many witnesses depicted as mandalas. We have found that the mandalas bring the pure energy of the witness into focus, and work very well.

The position of the elements is important. The earth-water placement creates an energy line between them that goes through the center of the circle. A similar line is created between fire and air. This placement becomes dual two-pole (or a four-pole) magnets that allow creation to occur. One two pole magnet is formed by the earth-water placement. The other magnet is formed by the fire-air placement. If air and fire are transposed the manifestation still works. However it is an energy that breaks up in order to put together. If the suggested placement is used the manifestation occurs through attraction. The directions do not need to be deliberately placed. They are always present so just honoring them when the site is dedicated is enough to invoke their presence.

The following definitions of the elements don't by any means invalidate the periodic table of the elements so well known by physicists. Instead, these are the metaphysical definitions used since ancient times for describing the energies that allow manifestation to occur.

Air: Creates the Space needed for manifestation.
Fire: Creates the movement needed for manifestation.
Water: Creates the contraction needed for manifestation.
Earth: Creates the solidity that is manifested.

In order to be complete concerning the fundamental energies we should also describe the four winds. The four winds are movements associated with the four directions. Although they are not specifically employed in the creation of the sacred site, they are active whenever a decision for action is present. They are also present whenever a thought is formed.

North Wind: The pause to assimilate
South Wind: Active & innocent learning.
West Wind: Stimulation toward movement.
East Wind: An awakening about the future.

Using the Sacred Site

Over the years we have found that by following the following steps, your interaction and understanding of a sacred site will be greatly enhanced. Everybody has differently tuned senses. Some people see pictures while others just experience feelings. Many people will not seem to get anything. However, their subconscious will always hold the experience. It is just a matter of time before the information can be accessed. Above all else, remember to respect the site, it's guardians and the energies.

Observe the physical site.

If at all possible, walk the perimeter of the site without getting close to what are obviously the physical structures. However, carefully observe the physical placement of all the structures and their alignments. This will give you a general feel of the site.

Find the entrance.

The entrance that you are looking for is not the entrance to a building, etc. It is the entrance to the entire area the site occupies. It can always be found by locating two objects such as trees, rocks, hedges or perhaps just an indent in the ground. The entrance is a gateway through the bounding area of what is outside and what is inside the site. You will be able to clearly feel the difference between energies at the site's boundary.

Contact the spirit guardian.

Stand just before the entrance and scribe the protective circles around you. The method of scribing the circles is found in the previous chapter. Then call the guardian into your circles stating that you want to work with the site in order to understand it's energy and it's use.

Ask permission to interact with the site.

When you feel the etheric presence of the guardian (in about one minute) ask permission to enter. The guardian will always consent to you entering, however, there often will be some questions asked about your intent. Even though permission is granted there is no guarantee as to what information will be made available to you. The information depends upon your true intent, your need to know and how you will use the site.

Walk the physical site.

Now it is possible to walk any portions of the site you are drawn to. Be patient and pause often in order to get the full realization of the site. It is always a good idea to contemplate or meditate often in order to recognize the etheric, as well as the physical nature of the site.

Meditate with the spirit guardian.

At some place along your walk you will be drawn to a particular spot that seems to have a stronger, more balanced energy. This would be a good spot to stop and meditate with the site's guardian. Be sure to ask the guardian as to the site's purpose remembering that the site may have been used differently over the years.

Thank the guardian.

At the end of you visit, walk back to the entrance and pause long enough to thank the site and the guardian for the visit and the information.

Creating and Using the Petal Pattern

Personal Petal Patterns

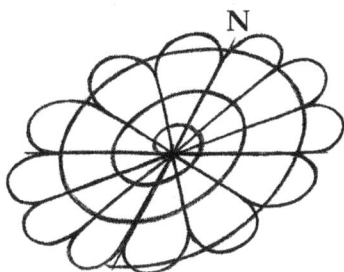

A Petal Pattern can be created to be used for personal problem solving and insight. Naturally the Petal Pattern is present in every object or living thing. However, creating an independent Petal Pattern brings focus to the pattern's ability to understand the old while allowing new to enter.

To create a Petal Pattern:

1. Create a sacred site that encloses the area that is going to be used.

2. Draw a useful sized picture of the Petal Pattern with its Spiral within the space. Make sure the pattern is properly laid out according the cardinal directions with the start of the Spiral in the West.

3. Holding a witness card, (perhaps healing or questions) dedicate the Space to the purpose you want the pattern to achieve. Place the card in the center.

4. Place the four Elemental Energies in their proper alignment outside of the pattern but inside the sacred site. With each elemental energy say "I place this energy to manifest the purpose of this Petal Pattern."

5. Thank the energies for their use and their purpose.

To use the Petal Pattern for insight:

1. Re-establish the sacred site by scribing the circles.

2. Enter the sacred site from the East.

3. While standing at the West end of the Spiral, bring your question or reason for using the pattern into your mind.

4. Release your thoughts and walk the Spiral to its center. Pause at each of the twelve petals during each of the three

loops of the Spiral until you feel that it is time to move on. Each pause can last for five seconds to a minute or more.

5. Pause for a bit in the center to reflect, contemplate or meditate on what has occurred.

6. Reverse direction and walk the Spiral back to it's start.

7. Thank the Petal Pattern for its interaction and its help.

8. Release the sacred site.

That's it. As you walk the Spiral, keep yourself in a quiet, receptive mood, and pause when you feel a need to stop. This allows the Universe to do its work.

To re-dedicate the Petal Pattern:

1. Enter the sacred site from the East and, standing in the center, pick up the witness that describes the patterns purpose, and thank it for its work and its help.

2. Call the Foundation Energies and say that they no longer manifest the old purpose of the Petal Pattern.

3. Place the witness outside the East entrance of the sacred site and bring a new witness to the center of the Petal Pattern.

4. Repeat steps three on of dedication and placement of the Elemental Energies in order to manifest the new purpose.

The new purpose is now ready to be used.

Practicality

Petal Pattern for Release

The Petal Pattern provides an extremely useful tool for releasing old thoughts, habits or anything physical that is no longer needed. We have found it particularly powerful for releasing a physical possession like a house or automobile that needs to be sold. The Petal Pattern helps release the old object while simultaneously readying it for the new owner.

All that you need to do is the following:

1. Locate the Petal Pattern for whatever you want to release. For personal thoughts, etc. it will be your physical bodies Petal Pattern. Your pattern is usually just in front of yourself. The pattern for an object can be located by dowsing. If you are using your Petal Pattern just tell it to stay in one place. It will then stay anchored, even when you step aside for the process.

2. Clearly bring to mind whatever you want to change or release.

3. Step into the first petal (physical internalization) that is just below due west, and say "I release whatever is necessary and bring in whatever is needed in order to accomplish this change."

4. Repeat step three for the remaining eleven petals, being sure to pause at each petal long enough to feel the release and acceptance.

5. When you are finished, thank the energies for their work.

That's it! With enough acceptance the result will be amazing.

The Labyrinth

Whenever a labyrinth is created the Universe also creates a Petal Pattern. The Petal Pattern overlays the labyrinth and provides interaction with the labyrinth walker. So, in reality, to create a Petal Pattern, all that needs to be done is to create a Labyrinth.

What the labyrinth does is to provide a path that passes through all the energies of the Petal Pattern. The simplest of all labyrinths is probably the most effective because there is a pure, direct relationship between the walker and the Universe.

Many excellent books on labyrinths already exist. This chapter cuts right to the origin energies and explains how to create a Petal Pattern that can be used as a labyrinth. There is no problem if you want to create a Petal Pattern and then place a traditional labyrinth of your choice over it.

Manifestation & the Laniscate

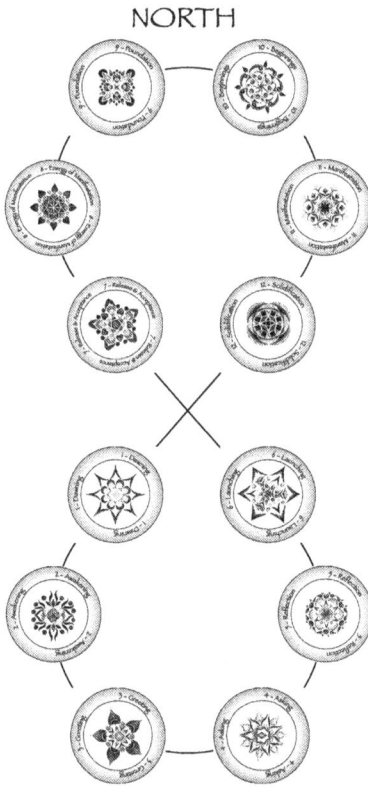

NORTH

The Laniscate is used in the same way as you would use one of the Wisdom maps.

The Laniscate is particularly good to aid the process of manifestation. What you manifest can be something physical, such as a new job, or something more mental, such as an attitude re-alignment associated with some issue you are facing. The Laniscate is also particularly good at manifesting wholeness.

To create a Laniscate just follow these steps:

1. Create a sacred site that encloses the area that is going to be used for the Laniscate.

2. Dedicate the Space to hold a Laniscate.

3. Place the Laniscate discs in their appropriate place in a figure eight manner within the sacred site. Make sure the Laniscate is aligned North - South.

4. Place the Elemental Energies to manifest the energy of the Laniscate.

To use the Laniscate do the following:

1. Enter the sacred site from the East.

2. While standing at the East, bring your question or reason for using the Laniscate into your mind.

3. Release your thoughts and move to its center.

4. Walk the Laniscate following the numeric order of the disks. If you feel a need to pause, stand for a bit until the energies are integrated.

5. Pause for a bit at the cross point in the center to reflect,

contemplate or meditate on what has occurred.

    6. Thank the Laniscate for its interaction and its help.

    7. Release the sacred site.

Manifestation Maps for the Laniscate

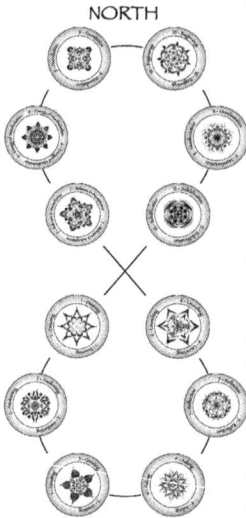

NORTH

The Laniscate can be used as a tool for manifestation. It doesn't matter weather the manifestation is the answer to a question, the solution for an issue or a new Ferrari. The Universe treats all equally. However, belief, focus and intent matter!

    To use the Laniscate for manifestation first clearly bring whatever you want to manifest into your mind. Next walk the Laniscate, pausing at each of the 12 stations (or the 12 energies of the Laniscate) long enough to feel the energy 'lock in.' The Laniscate is walked following the order of the cards first with the introspective counter-clockwise south loop and then the active clockwise loop.

    The order to walk the Laniscate is as follows:

1. Dawning	2. Awakening
3. Greeting	4. Asking
5. Reflection	6. Launching
7. Release and Acceptance	8. Energy of Manifestation
9. Foundation	10. Beginnings
11. Manifestation	12. Solidification

Practicality

Problem Solving Map for the Laniscate

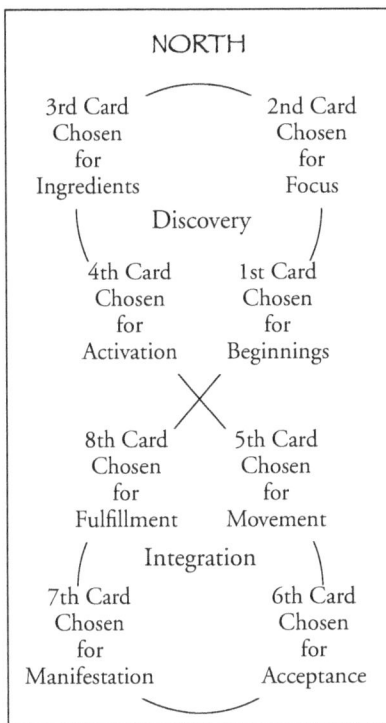

```
                    NORTH

  3rd Card                    2nd Card
  Chosen                      Chosen
   for                          for
 Ingredients                  Focus
            \    Discovery    /
    4th Card        1st Card
    Chosen          Chosen
      for             for
  Activation        Beginnings

              X

  8th Card        5th Card
  Chosen          Chosen
    for             for
 Fulfillment      Movement
        /   Integration   \
  7th Card                    6th Card
  Chosen                      Chosen
    for                         for
 Manifestation               Acceptance
```

Another way the Laniscate can be used in problem solving is for you to personally select the energies that best help you in understanding the situation. Then apply them to a walk around the Laniscate to manifest the answer.

First, select eight cards that represent the following points on the abbreviated Laniscate.

1. Beginnings. This is the energy that will get you started.

2. Focus. This energy will clarify and focus your thoughts concerning the problem.

3. Ingredients. This energy will help bring everything needed for the solution together.

4. Activation. This energy will get the process ready.

5. Movement. This will get the process moving.

6. Acceptance. This energy will help you to accept the solution.

7. Manifestation. This will manifest the solution.

8. Fulfillment. This energy will help you feel good about the accomplishment.

Next lay out the cards in the prescribed order and walk the Laniscate being sure to pause at each step or energy. Start with the north loop walking it in a counter-clockwise manner. This is the loop of Receptive Internal Discovery.

Next walk the south loop of Active External Manifestation. If the direction that you walk the loops seems strange, give it a chance anyway. We have found that it will work powerfully.

Creating & Using a Wisdom Circle

This section gives a detailed description of how the twelve energies of the Wisdom Circle can be used. As you go over these energies remember that they represent arenas which create a Space to bring wisdom into any question, issue or stated purpose. These energies are not like Tarot cards which give answers to questions. Instead, they create an attitude or Space that can give birth to the answer. The Space is mental in nature, so with a bit of practice, the Wisdom Circle can become a source of spiritual wisdom to aid in any aspect of growth. Through experience we have found that interaction with a Wisdom Circle can bring about life changing perspectives. The guidance of the Wisdom Circle does this in a gentle, purposeful way.

Even though the Wisdom Circle is part of the Complex of Clarity, it can be created as a separate sacred site.

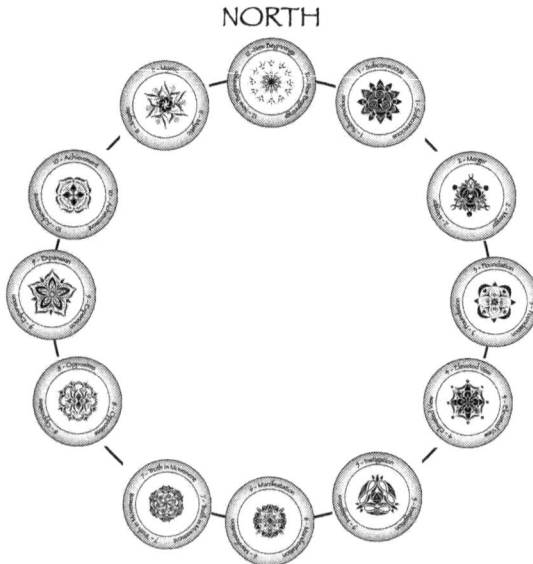

NORTH

When the Wisdom Circle is separately established it becomes the physical sacred site. Therefore a full set of etheric structures that are associated with any sacred site are established and attached to the physical Wisdom Circle. This even includes a Wisdom Circle for the Wisdom Circle!

Well, it's best to ignore the complexities of the matter and look at the creation of a physical Wisdom Circle and how it can be used.

To create a Wisdom Circle just follow these steps:

1. Create a sacred site that encloses the area that is going to be used for the Wisdom Circle.
2. Dedicate the Space to hold a Wisdom Circle.
3. Place the wisdom discs in their appropriate place in a circle within the sacred site. Make sure that the North - South and East - West alignment is accurate.
4. Place the Elemental Energies to manifest the energy of the Wisdom Circle.

There are two major ways to make use of the Wisdom Circle. To use it in either way do the following:

1. Enter the sacred site from the East.
2. While standing facing the North, bring your question or reason for using the Wisdom Circle into your mind.
3. Release your thoughts and move to its center.
4. This step depends on which mode of use you prefer. See descriptions A and B which follow and then continue with step 5.
5. Pause for a bit in the center to reflect, contemplate or meditate on what has occurred.
6. Thank the Wisdom Circle for its interaction and its help and leave to the East.
7. Release the sacred site.

A: The first way is the simplest. You stand in the center of the circle and slowly turn in a counter clock wise direction until you feel a need to pause. You stop and contemplate for a moment to receive whatever information the Wisdom Circle has to offer. Then turn 180° and receive what the polarity energy has to tell you. Then you repeat that step by continuing to turn, stopping when you feel a need. You will usually stop two or three times in order to gain the complete effect.

When you stop you will be facing a wisdom disk and its polarity disk at your back. The energy of the disk interacts with you in a way that imparts wisdom to the question or issue you are working with. Be prepared for a new perspective or idea. After all, if you knew the answer or the answer followed traditional logic you wouldn't be here, would you?

Wisdom Circle Maps

B: The second way is a bit more complex, but provides greater flexibility to the process. First you choose one of the four maps that follow. The maps represent:

1. The Six Dual Maps of Inner Movement. This is a good map for internal realizations such as emotional issues, etc.

2. The Four Triad Maps of Bridging. This map works well with matters that need interaction with another person or situation such as a job or anything that is outside of yourself.

3. The Three Quad Maps of Outer Movements. This map helps you to step outside of yourself in order to look at situations that require a change of direction. It helps you to find a new perspective about something that is beyond yourself.

4. The Two Sextile Maps of Regeneration. This map is great for healing or to completely change your perspective about any situation.

To use the maps just place the wisdom disks on the ground in the positions shown. Then walk between each disk of a group as shown by the small arrows, staying open and aware of any information or energy movement that occurred. After each group is completed pause while standing in the center for as long as you need in order to assimilate the energy. Then walk to the next group as indicated by the large arrow.

Practicality

The Six Dual Maps of Inner Movement
(Inner Realizations)

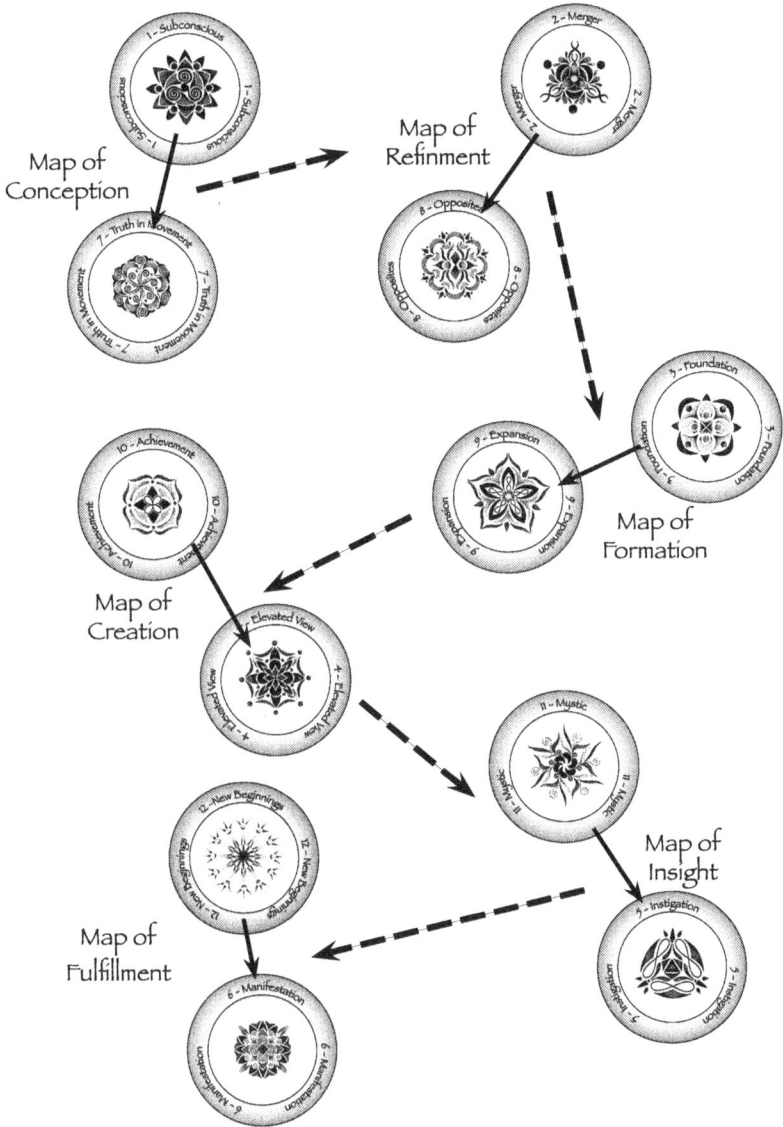

Map of
Conception

Map of
Refinment

Map of
Formation

Map of
Creation

Map of
Insight

Map of
Fulfillment

1 - Subconscious

2 - Merger

7 - Truth in Movement

8 - Opposites

3 - Foundation

9 - Expansion

10 - Achievement

4 - Elevated View

11 - Mystic

12 - New Beginnings

5 - Instigation

6 - Manifestation

The Four Triad Maps of Bridging
(Interact with a Situation)

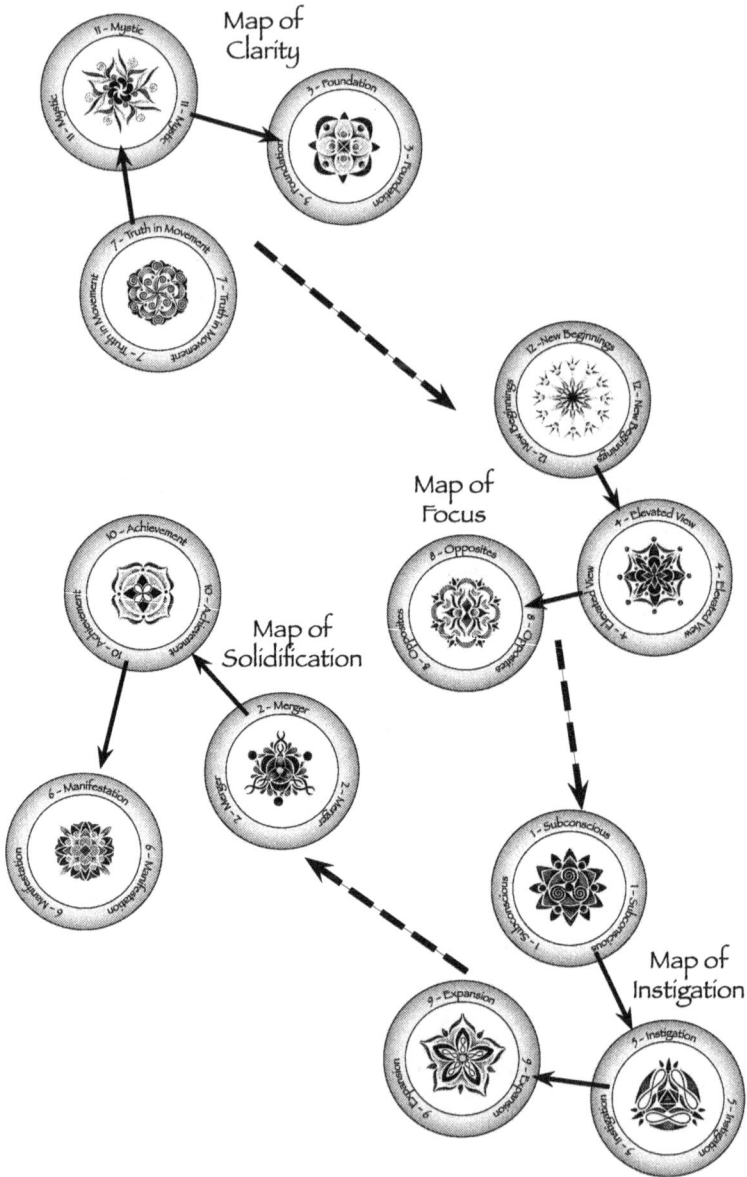

Map of
Clarity

Map of
Focus

Map of
Solidification

Map of
Instigation

Practicality

The Three Quad Maps of Movements
(New Perspective)

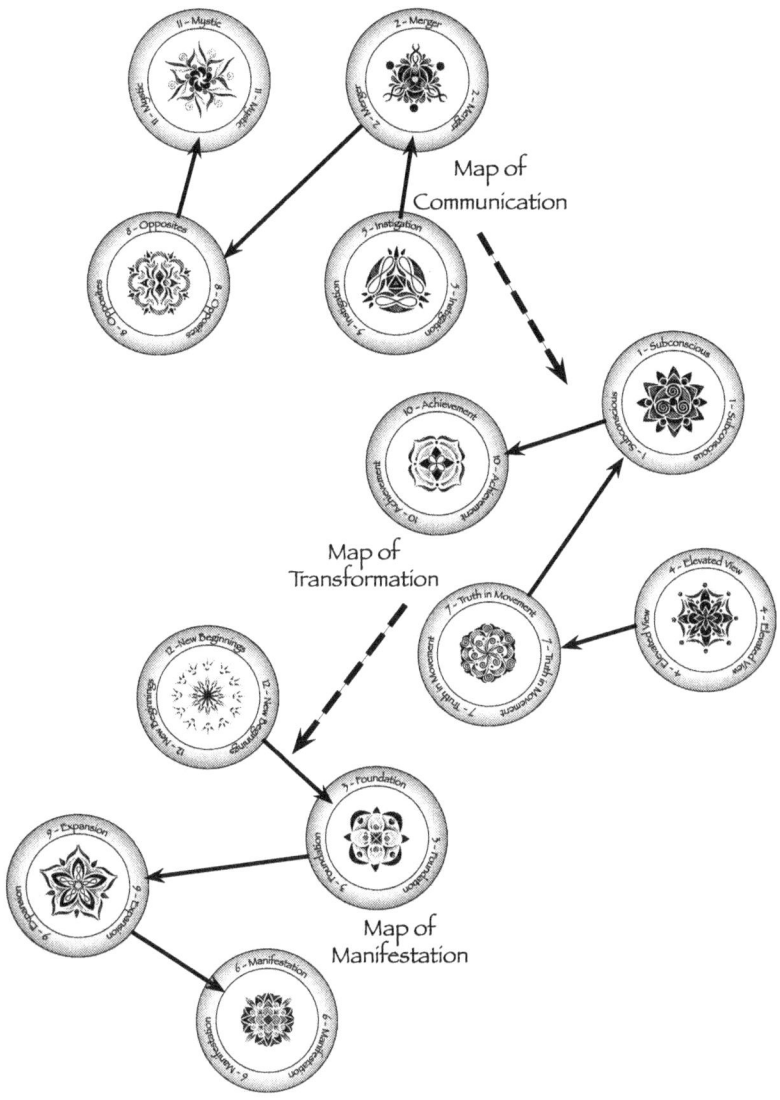

The Two Sextile Maps of Regeneration
(Healing)

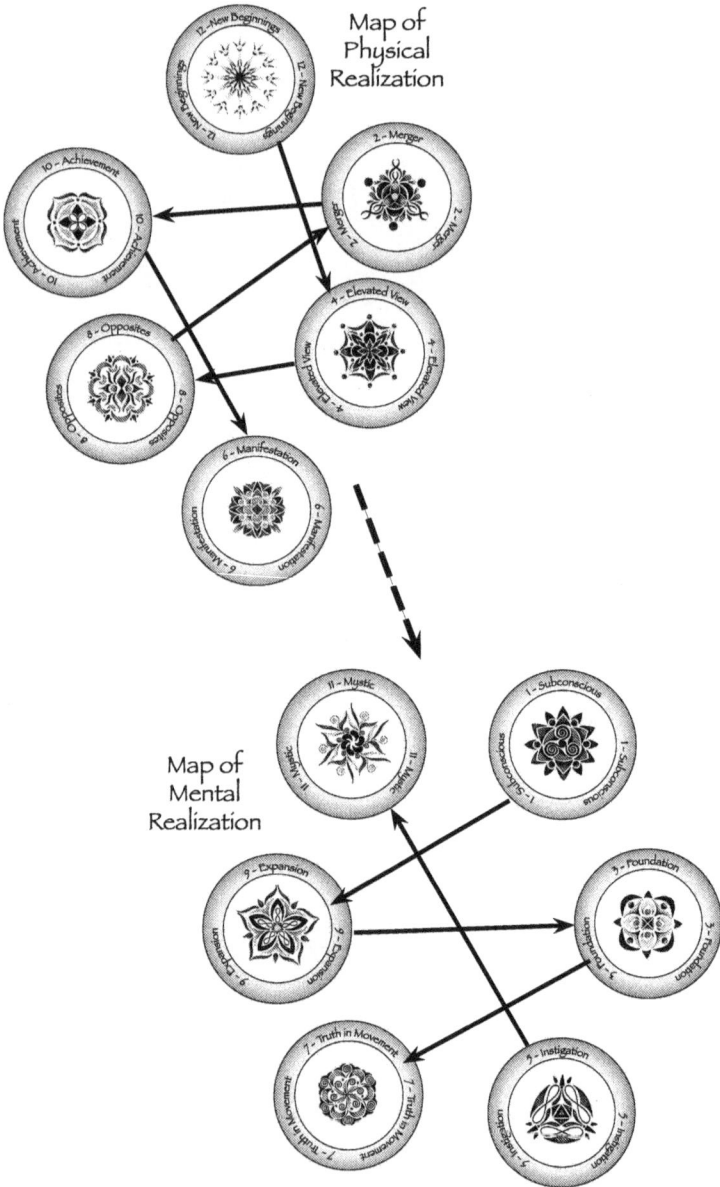

Map of
Physical
Realization

Map of
Mental
Realization

Creating and Using an Altar

An altar is a classical sacred site and has all the etheric components associated with sacred site's as part of its energy. Therefore, the steps for creating an altar are identical to Chapter Five's descriptions for creating any sacred site.

The basic components of an altar include a central candle that represents the creative force, and surrounding the central candle, a representation of the four elements. These five items are contained within a circle. Anything else that is placed on an altar adds to its energy but does not add to its function other than to provide a more focused purpose.

To create an altar just follow these steps.

1. Create a sacred site that encloses the area that is going to be used for the altar.

2. Place within the sacred circle a circular table or draw a physical circle on whatever the icons are going to be placed upon.

3. Dedicate the altar using and placing the central candle in the center of the circle.

4. Place the Elemental Energies on the indicated positions to manifest the purpose of the altar. Earth is in the North-West. Water is in the South-East. Fire is in the South-West. Air is in the North-East.

To use the altar follow these basic steps:

1. Always recreate the sacred site around the existing altar. Then enter the sacred site from the East.

2. Light the central candle first and the elemental candle from the central candle. As you light the candles, call upon those energies that will be helpful on whatever the altar is going to be used for.

3. When you are finished, blow out the elemental candle and then the central candle.

4. After finishing with any individual use of the altar, release the Space back to its origin energies. This does not diminish the power of the altar it simply shows respect for the energies and prepares them for your next use.

It is a good idea to always light the central candle from a taper that is reserved solely for that purpose. Just before the taper is used up, light a new taper from the old one. This will transfer the original energy forward and helps to maintain the altar's power.

Using the Universal Connection

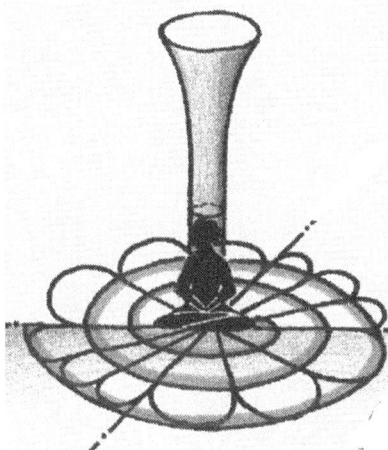

The Universal Connection is the link to the Universe. The Pulse, that is created by the Four Pole Magnet, is the heartbeat that locks in the connection. When the magnet is recognized to be in the center of the Petal Pattern the entire structure becomes a real powerhouse for inner personal insight and change. Everything together creates a consistent, clear and wise link to everything that ever was, is or will be at a level that can be personally understood. Sounds like a big order doesn't it?

To use the Universal connection follow these steps:

1. Create a sacred site that encloses the area that is going to be used.

2. Dedicate the Space to hold a Universal Connection.

3. Enter the sacred site from the East.

4. While standing facing the North, bring your question or reason for using the Wisdom Circle into your mind.

5. Release your thoughts and move to its center.

6. Sit and meditate allowing a higher interaction to occur.

7. When finished, thank the Universal connection for its interaction and its help and leave to the East.

8. Release the sacred site.

Naturally, using the connection requires some practice but the link is a natural extension of the meditative process so it doesn't take too long to get the hang of it.

Using Pyramid Energy

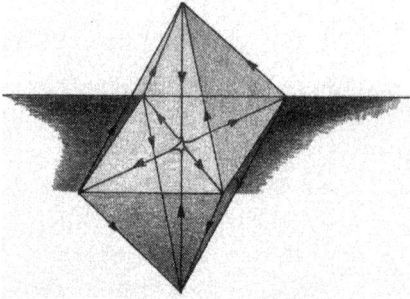

The structure of Pyramids recirculate energy. This means that anyone sitting in the Pyramid will have their thoughts recirculated. This creates either a focus or a chaotic mix of thoughts depending upon how centered you are. Therefore it is doubly important to create a sacred site in which the Pyramid is used. Also be sure to scribe the purifying and protective circles before each use. A good way to represent the Pyramid is by creating a wire frame model of the top part that sits on the Earth. The part that reaches into the Earth will be automatically created by the Universe. The Pyramid is not dangerous but it's nice to use it in a productive, centered and focused manner.

Using the Pyramid is simplicity itself. Scribe your circles and then just sit in the center making sure you are focused. Then meditate in the style that is comfortable for you. You will find that your meditations are clearer and more focused.

The Pyramid reaches into the earth as well into the etheric world. Therefore, when you are centered, you will feel a stretching movement that anchors yourself. Use the stretch as a tool to connect the wisdom of the spiritual world with the practicality of the Earth by saying "I connect the two worlds to bring wisdom and balance to myself, the Earth and all humanity." This means that everything benefits from the meditation.

Using Cube of Space Energy

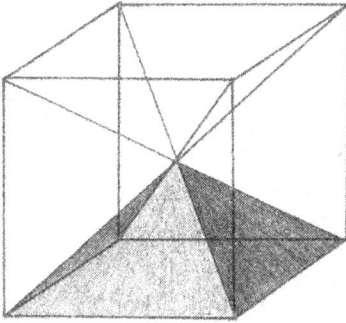

The Cube of Space is like a halfway house between the spirit and physical worlds. It is where formation occurs, be it a thought or a solid object. The Cube is a great place to meditate whenever you want to clarify your thoughts or to get started on a project or a manifestation.

Using the Cube is similar to using the Pyramid. Start by creating a wire frame model of the structure that is sized so you can sit in it with your solar plexus in the exact center of the Cube. Then create a sacred site by scribing your circles and dedicate the Space to the Cube. Then sit in its center for meditation. You will receive clear, strong insights and, who knows, a solid object may appear.

Using the Foundation Energies

Elements for Manifestation

Meditating on the elements by following a path starting at the lightest (air) then going step wise to the heaviest (Fire, Water and Earth) are a great help in bringing all the necessary ingredients together for manifestation.

It is important to feel or become each element as you progress along the meditation. A good way to do this is to visualize the element in its natural physical state. Try following a path that starts out in the forest then by a stream or pool of water, then to the warmth of a beach and then to a high mountain. The path touches all elements in a familiar manner and makes the spirit connection more physical. After all, manifestation bridges the spirit and physical worlds.

Directions for Problem Solving

The directions provide the perspectives necessary for manifestation and clarity. The process is straightforward:

1, Scribe the circles to create a purified and protected space.

2. Begin to meditate by bringing whatever it is that you wish to understand better into your mind.

3. Take the thought to the North to see it in its wise overview.

4. Then take the thought to the South to see the innocent details.

5. Then to the West in order to see and instigate the solution.

6. Finally to the East to see the full solution and its ramifications over the long haul.

Practicality

Winds for Movement

The winds create the flow and power to accomplish a transformation. Their action is controlled by thought. The winds can be used in a manner similar to the directions.

1, Scribe the circles to create a purified and protected space.

2. Begin to meditate by bringing whatever it is that you wish to change into your mind.

3. First call upon the East Wind to awaken yourself to the true nature of the situation.

4. Then call upon the South Wind to stabilize your feelings about the situation without dropping back into an old pattern.

5. Then call upon the West Wind to stimulate you into enthusiastic action.

6. Finally call upon the North Wind to assimilate what you have learned.

Summary

Sacred sites exist everywhere there is a need for an Universal connection. This means that there are literally millions of sacred sites scattered throughout the world. A sacred site is actually a complex of etheric structures that support, maintain and anchor the energies of the Space in a manner which can be felt. These etheric structures include: a double ended Pyramid of Perpetuation which anchors the energies; a Clarity Complex which maintains a pure identity for the site; and an Interaction Complex which provides an Universal link, connecting the user of the site with the wisdom of the Universe.

A sacred site is created as follows:
• First a sacred circle is scribed to purifies and protect the space.
• Then a purpose is defined and the directions are honored. This gives expression to the purpose of the space.
• Then the Elemental Energies are placed, manifesting the purpose of the space.
• Finally any physical work needed to build the Space is done.
Then the Universe creates:
• A Pyramid that perpetuates and anchors the purpose;
• A Clarification Complex that maintains the expression of the purpose.
• An Interaction Complex that interactively bridges the expression of the space's purpose with the user of the site.

The Wisdom Circle can be created as a sacred site. The resulting site allows the user to formulate answers to questions or to access energy that heals. The answer or healing energy has origins within the creative force. Additionally, a Petal Pattern can be created as an independent sacred site. That site provides interaction between the meditative state and the Universe in a clear concise way.
The Earth is a perfect example of a sacred site, where each element of a sacred site is reproduced on a giant scale. A small

icon, such as a ring, has all of the elements of a sacred site on a minute scale. The Earth repeats the same elements on a giant scale.

There is strong evidence that the same patterns are reproduced on a Universal scale. This repetition of sacred sites throughout the Earth and the Universe creates a structure that is in constant movement and in communication with everything within the Universe. In that sense, the energies of sacred sites creates what many call the Universal mind.

It is possible to place yourself at any of the millions of sacred sites and achieve, through meditation, an interaction with any other sacred site in the Universe.

Part IV Divination

This book is accompanied by a set of divination cards which depict the Universal energies. The cards can be easily used by anyone who wants to touch three levels of consciousness. They are:

1. Physical: Obtain a direct answer to questions. This is the mundane, or personal perspective.

2. Mental: An attitude is created that allows the answer to be discovered through your own attunement. This is the discovery perspective.

3. Spiritual: An arena is created in which the answer is manifested. This is the perspective that brings the answer into your life in a way that supports your growth process.

Using these cards can provide you with unique opportunities for divination and subsequent growth. For example, a spread can be chosen that brings you a direct answer to your question (physical), or an answer that is conjured up from your own intuitive skills (mental), or an answer that becomes active through your own journey (spiritual).

Naturally, the level of use you choose is important. Sometimes it might seem easier to go for the direct answer. However, remember that the point to life is to grow spiritually and experience the life path you choose via your free will choices. Our advice to you is to go for it and allow the mental and spiritual divination spreads to work for you in a way that brings interesting opportunities along the way. Accepting and working with the opportunities will become part of your path of growth and fulfillment.

You might find yourself starting with the physical interpretation, and then later be pushed toward the mental and spiritual interpretations. The best time to make this type of switch will be found in your answers. If your answers migrate toward inconclusiveness, move to the higher frequencies of the mental and spiritual interpretations. You will always find your own best teacher, yourself, is pushing you in the right direction.

Divination

The card deck is your own personal sacred site. It becomes yours personally through its use. In fact, each card of the deck is actually a personal sacred site. Each card draws you to the answer that is uniquely best for you, not only from a perspective that is understandable by you, but also from the point of view that your path is your own sacred journey and the journey itself is your reward.

All of the cards in this deck depict a fundamental Universal energy that, by its inability to be subdivided into more basic forms, is pure. In order to retain that purity we have kept the definitions somewhat esoteric. Our hope is that those who are interested will build upon this deck to create new decks that depict the energies toward more finely tuned uses.

That is not to say that these cards are impractical. On the contrary, some of the most useful advice we have gathered has come through the use of these cards and the spreads described in this book. However, as you use these cards, be prepared for pure and direct advice that has origin from within the Universe.

The power of the cards is amplified through use, and the mandalas and descriptions become more and more powerful as time goes on. Best wishes on your path. We hope that these cards are of some help to you!

Universal Energies

We call the energies Universal because they represent the origin energies of the creative process. They are not hampered by an ego based bias. They are simply energies that have the potential to help in the process of being human. In fact, they don't care how you use them. They will work with you at whatever level or purpose you choose.

Because these are unique origin energies they cannot be logically divided into sub categories or smaller pieces. This means that when they are used for divination, the heart of the answer is presented. Or, in other words, there is nothing hidden behind the energies and therefore hidden in the answer. This is good news if you have been barking up the wrong tree for awhile and are truly interested in a new way of looking at a question or issue. This is hopefully the normal case, or why would you spend good money and use valuable time to find an answer? Remember that it is just as easy to move forward as to stay stuck in an old perspective. Be open to what is indicated.

The Universal energies can be divided into four categories:

1. The Foundation Energies

These are the building blocks of the Universe and represent all the ingredients needed for manifestation. Individually these twelve energies are; Directions which represent perspectives. Elements which represent ingredients, and Winds which represent movements. They are:

Directions	Elements	Winds
North	Earth	North Wind
South	Water	South Wind
West	Fire	West Wind
East.	Air.	East Wind

2. The Wisdom Energies

These are the twelve divisions of the unfoldment of wisdom where each division represents a step along the way on the path of understanding. Individually they are:

1. New Beginnings	7. Manifestation
2. Subconscious	8. Truth in Movement
3. Merger	9. Opposites
4. Foundation	10. Expansion
5. Elevated View	11. Achievement
6. Instigation	12. Mystic

3. The Laniscate Energies

These are the twelve steps of manifestation, be it the manifestation of a pot of gold, or an idea. Individually they are:

1. Dawning	7. Release and Acceptance
2. Awakening	8. Energy of Manifestation
3. Greeting	9. Foundation
4. Asking	10. Beginnings
5. Reflection	11. Manifestation
6. Launching	12. Solidity

4. The Receptacle Energies

These are the twelve divisions of bridging, and they represent the ways the Universe can interact and be observed. Individually they are:

1. Physical Internalization	7. Physical Interaction
2. Mental Internalization	8. Mental Interaction
3. Spiritual Internalization	9. Spiritual Interaction
4. Spiritual Integration	10. Spiritual Dispersement
5. Mental Integration	11. Mental Dispersement
6. Physical Integration	12. Physical Dispersement

In addition, two other classes of energies have been included. These energies are not necessarily fundamental Universal energies, but they help obtain clearer answers by "rounding out" the divination deck.

They are:
5. The Witness Energies:
These represent seven needs or conditions.

6. The Growth Energies:
These represent five milestones toward growth.

Individually these twelve energies are:

The Witness Energies	The Growth Energies
1. Manifestation	1. The Inward Funnel
2. Healing	2. The Outward Funnel
3. Questions	3. The Stepping Stones
4. Introspection	4. The Seed
5. Communication	5. The Bridge
6. Rejuvenation	
7. Peace	

Note that Manifestation appears in the Wisdom, Laniscate and Witness categories. Thus the three Manifestation cards each refer back to their category and represent important differences. The Wisdom Manifestation represents the concept of manifestation. The Laniscate Manifestation represents a step in the process of manifestation. The Witness Manifestation represents the need to manifest.

The Care and Feeding of Your Cards

In order to most effectively use the cards for divination (i.e. to get direct useful answers) it is helpful to follow these guidelines:

1. Respect

The more the cards are respected, the more powerful they become. Respect, at the very least, means recognizing and thanking the energies each time the cards are used. Even though the energies don't have a personality or need for recognition, they are alive and growing. The vitality of your cards will be more clearly felt when the cards are respected and used. The card's power comes from a realization that, through use, something good will come from it.

2. Friendship

Friendship involves the most productive interaction possible between two sentient beings. In friendship there are no strings attached. In true friendship there is no "If I scratch your back, you will scratch mine." Friendship is not easy to maintain. Egos seem to get in the way of a purer form of interaction. True friendship is an interaction that involves complete trust and faith in each other.

Your cards are sentient. They have a purpose and a life that desires communication and honesty. They don't have an ego that says "I know more than you." They just have a desire to help. Now, what greater friendship can there be!

One way to become friends with your deck is to give it a name. We have named ours and it seems to like it. We also don't allow other people to use our cards. They are our personal friend and we don't want other people's energy entering this Space and confusing our communications.

3. Protection

Your cards should be protected at all times. This is not only to show respect, but also keeps them in a Space that is easy to use and understand. The water isn't muddied, so-to-speak.

Protection comes from keeping them wrapped in an appropriate cloth, placed in a bag or container and hidden away when not in use.

4. Use

The more you use the cards, the happier they are. And, the more you use them the more accurately you can decipher them. Also, use creates a deeper personal understanding of the cards that makes divination easier. Finally show a respect that says "You are of value to me."

5. Creating a Sacred Site

The first step in preparing for divination is to create a sacred circle of purification and protection around the area where the divination is to be performed. The circle can be created mentally, temperately, or permanently as described in the section about scribing circles. Repeating the sacred circle process each time the cards are used will increase their power and usefulness enormously.

To create a temporary sacred site follow these steps:

1 - Choose a Space or table surface that is good for the divination that you will be doing.

2 - While mentally scribing (drawing) a counter-clockwise circle 3 times around the space, say: "I call upon the powers of the Heaven and the Earth to merge and mix, purifying this space."

When finished say: "Thank you powers of the Heaven and Earth for purifying this space."

3 - Then mentally scribe a clockwise circle 3 times around the purified space, say: "I call upon the power of the Creative Force to protect this area."

When finished say: "Thank you power of the Creative Force for protecting this space."

Then say: "So be it!"

6. Clearly State the Question

There is nothing more important for a clear, concise answer than the way a question is stated. If a question is nebulous, the answer will also be nebulous. Make sure there are no obvious or hidden inconsistencies. The cards will work from the dictionary definitions of the words you use. Don't fall into the trap of saying "Well, the cards know what I mean." Yes the cards do know what you mean but they will answer the question as it is stated.

The best way to clarify a question is to write it down. Then examine what you have written and ask yourself "If I were a foreigner and I didn't understand this language, what would this question mean to me?" Also, make sure you are stating a single question. The cards can't answer more than one at a time. Keep refining the question until it states exactly what you want to ask, then proceed with the spread.

7. Perform the Divination

After respecting and protecting your cards, preparing the Space and making sure your question is clear, it is now time to perform the divination. We have included our favorite card spreads in the next chapter. However, any of your card spreads will also work, wether they come from tarot or from any other useful divination deck.

8. After the Divination

After you have completed your divination, thank the energies for their help and release the space. The energy of the sacred circle will stay around with use, but it will dissipate when not used. Not releasing the energies is a sign of disrespect. The release will not remove the energies; it only serves to return them to their source for rest. It is best to create and release the circle each time you need it. This keeps the energy fresh and powerful.

To release the Space after your work is finished, with an upward counter-clockwise motion of your hand, say: "I release the energies to their source. Thank you powers for the purification and the protection. So be it!"

9. Cleansing

After a lot of use, your cards will seem to get a bit sticky. Hopefully, not from last nights pizza, but rather because the energy of past divinations is sticking to them. When this happens, it is time to cleanse them.

There are two effective methods for cleaning the cards. The first is to place them out in the sun for about three hours. Make sure they are protected from random interference such as other people picking them up. The second way is to place them in a bag of salt for overnight.

Both ways work equally well. It's your choice which method you use. Of course the salt way works best on rainy days!

The Spreads and their Interpretation

The Nine Card Spread:
Three levels of understanding.

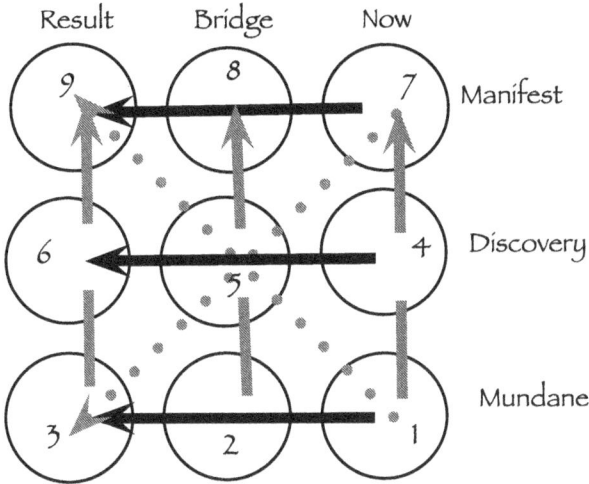

This spread gives three levels of understanding that brings a cohesive picture into an answer; mundane, discovery and manifest. The Mundane level gives a direct answer or process to follow concerning the question or issue. The discovery level gives the "what's in it for you" perspective. The Manifest level gives the steps necessary to bring growth into your life in relationship to the query.

The cards are laid out in the order indicated above. The right column indicates the present condition. The left column indicates the result. The middle column indicates the bridge between the current condition and the result.

This is an extremely useful spread and it is our personal favorite because of the amount of information it gives. Every question or issue we face in life has more purpose behind it than just curiosity or physical need. The nine card spread gives you the answer (the bottom row), how to apply the answer (the middle row), and how to bring the answer into your life (the top row).

The rows are read first from right to left. The columns can

also be read starting with the mundane and finishing with the manifest. They give refinements to the answer. In addition, the diagonals can be read. They help give a summary overview to the answer.

Here is an example of how we used the nine card spread as this book was being written back in September of 1999.

Question: What will be the results of people using this nine card spread?

Answer:

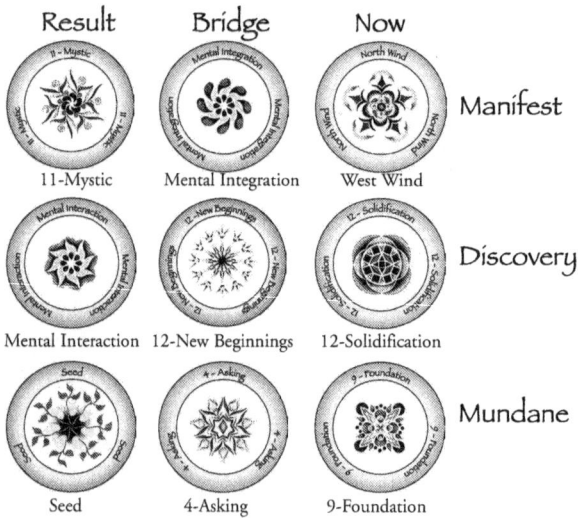

Result	Bridge	Now	
11-Mystic	Mental Integration	West Wind	Manifest
Mental Interaction	12-New Beginnings	12-Solidification	Discovery
Seed	4-Asking	9-Foundation	Mundane

Divination

Let's interpret this one row at a time starting with the mundane and finishing with the manifest.

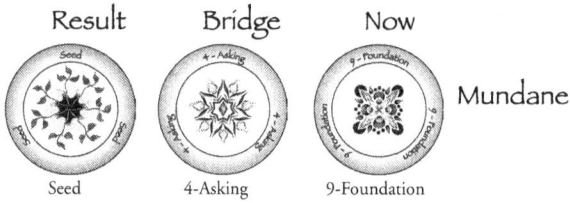

Result	Bridge	Now	
Seed	4-Asking	9-Foundation	Mundane

Now: 9 - Foundation: Ingredients of manifesting.
Bridge: 4 - Asking: Action toward movement.
Result: Seed: The new germ.

This is saying: Everything is present to bring the seed answer through physical activity (use).

Now the discovery level interpretation.

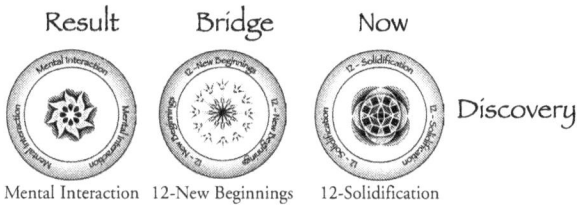

Result	Bridge	Now	
Mental Interaction	12-New Beginnings	12-Solidification	Discovery

Now: 12 - Solidification: Result of manifestation.
Bridge: 12 - New Beginnings: Newness dawns.
Result: Mental Interaction: Values.

This says: The results of the divination give new value through new information.

Lastly, the manifest level interpretation:

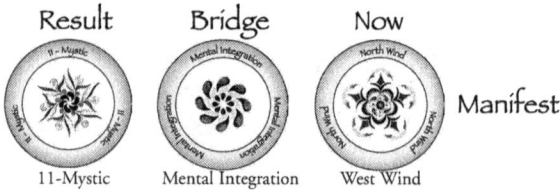

Result	Bridge	Now	
			Manifest
11-Mystic	Mental Integration	West Wind	

Now: West Wind: Stimulation.
Bridge: Mental Integration: Perception vs need.
Result: 11 - Mystic: Penetrate the veil.

This says: The resulting stimulation will give the ability to see the unseen through reality, not perceived need.

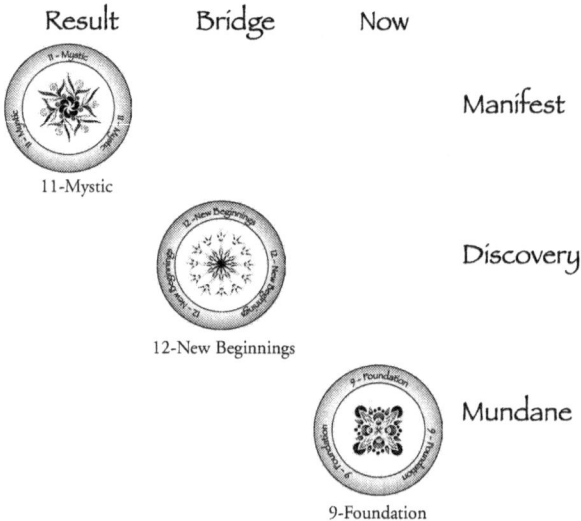

Result	Bridge	Now	
			Manifest
11-Mystic			
			Discovery
	12-New Beginnings		
			Mundane
		9-Foundation	

Let's also look at the diagonals. First, the current physical situation to the spiritual result.:

Now: 9 - Foundation: Ingredients of manifesting.
Bridge: 12 - New Beginnings: Newness dawns.
Result: 11 - Mystic: Penetrate the veil.

This says: The bridge to the all knowing answer rests in release of pre-conceived perceptions and rests in a strong foundation.

Now the other diagonal, from the physical result to the current manifest situation.

Result   Bridge   Now

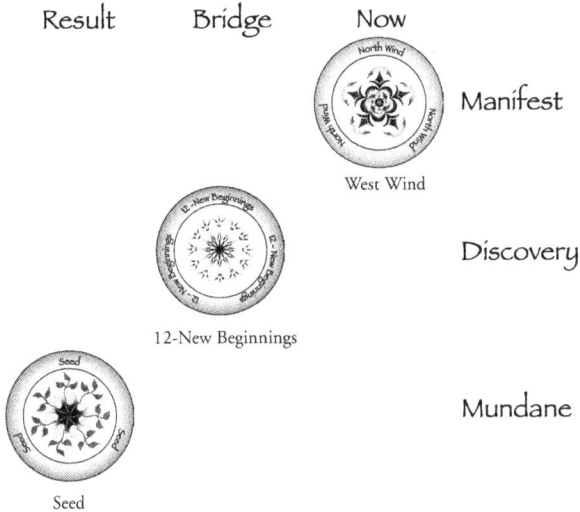

West Wind

Manifest

12-New Beginnings

Discovery

Seed

Mundane

Now: West Wind: Stimulation.
Bridge: 12 - New Beginnings: Newness dawns.
Result: Seed: The new germ.

This says: The mundane result of a seeded idea comes from a real stimulus that will use new concepts as a catalyst.

Now, what more could you ask of it? Well, how about timing and the future? These aspects are handled by other spreads described next.

The Seven Card Spread:
The steps toward resolution.

This spread shows seven steps that are necessary in order to produce the desired answer to a question. With this spread you begin at step one and proceed through step seven.

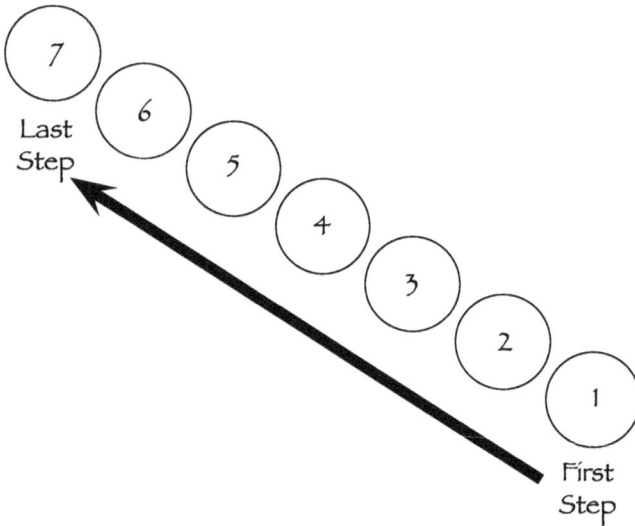

The cards are laid out and read in the order shown. Any one of the three interpretive levels (Mundane, Discovery or Manifest) can be used during the interpretation. Note that seven is the mystical number that corresponds to any realization or manifestation.

Divination

The following is an example of a seven card spread in October of 1999 when we were going to start interaction with publishers concerning publishing this book on Universal Divination.

The question was:

What do we need to do in order to publish this book?

The answer was:

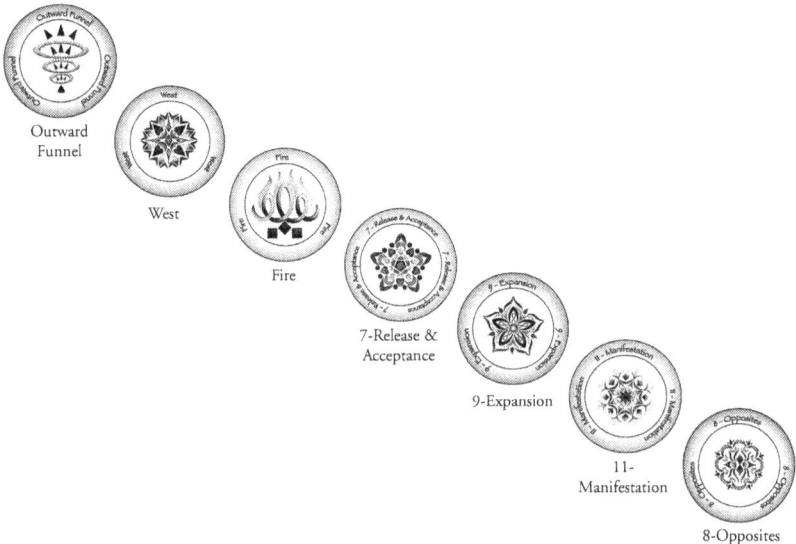

Outward Funnel

West

Fire

7-Release & Acceptance

9-Expansion

11-Manifestation

8-Opposites

The mundane description of the steps and interpretation was:

Step 1. 8 - Opposite's: The other side

Look at the process through the eyes of the publisher.

Step 2. 11 - Manifestation: Act of manifesting.

Finish the book.

Step 3. 9 - Expansion: Productive growth.

Put a presentation together for the publishers.

Step 4. 7 - Release & Acceptance:

Removal of pre-conceptions.

Send presentation out and accept what comes back.

Step 5. Fire: The movement.

Review comments and interact with the publishers.

Step 6. West: The active movement.

Decision on publisher and put together an agreement

Step 7. Outward Funnel: Inside out regeneration.

Make decisions and incorporate into final packaging.

The Six Card Spread
Universal Timing

Getting a handle on timing is an elusive task at best. In reality the Universe has no time other than natural order. It is we humans who demand to know when. However, when our time (our personal desire) happens to match Universal time, (Universal need) we drop into a synchronistic mode and things happen instantaneously.

So, the problem of resolving the time to manifest becomes a straight forward comparison of personal desire vs Universal need. This might sound simple except that personal desire easily becomes an ego oriented 'I want it my way'. It is the 'my way' attitude that leads to stubbornness and makes open mindedness difficult.

The six card spread is of enormous help in resolving conflicts between Universal and human timing. It does it by clearly comparing both in a way that shows us how to get in sync with the Universe. When the Universe and we are working together for the same result, timing either becomes zero or is unimportant.

Always keep an open mind. After all, you would not be reading this if you knew all the answers, would you!

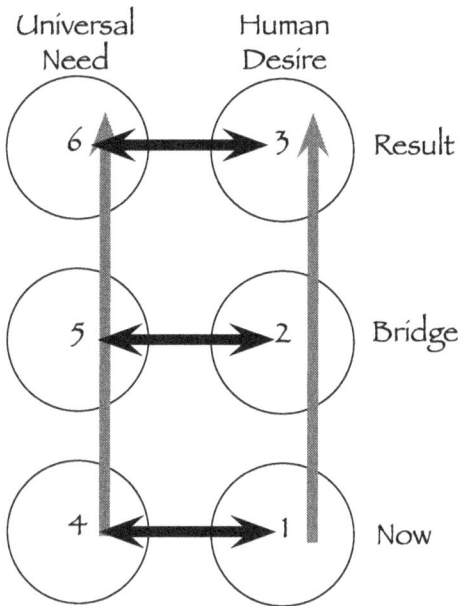

The cards are laid out in the order shown. Interpret the cards bottom to top starting with the human desire column then moving to the Universal need column. For additional insight look at the pairs 1/4, 2/5 and 3/6 to see where the Universe and you might differ.

If there is a lot of similarity, the timing is short. Dissimilar pares of energy show a lack of Universal synchronization and the timing will be further away. If the timing is unclear or too far out, go back to the nine card spread to see how to unscramble the issue.

Now lets look at an example of the six card spread:

The example question comes from 1999 when we were looking at publishing this book. We had already asked a question of the nine and seven card spreads (see previous examples) and we wanted to understand the timing a bit better.

The question was:
The timing for getting this book professionally published.
And the answer was:

Universal Need   Human Desire

Physical Dispersement   7-Release & Acceptance   Result

Spiritual Internalization   Spiritual Integration   Bridge

Stepping Stones   Peace   Now

Now let's interpret what we received...

Divination

First let's look at the human side...

Human
Desire

Now:
  Peace: Hold off chaos.
Bridge:
  Spiritual Integration: Environmental identity.
Result:
  7-Release & Acceptance: Release concepts.

We interpreted this as - Don't panic. The universe needs it, we just need to do our share.

Result

7-Release & Acceptance

Bridge

Spiritual Integration

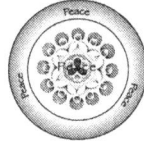

Now

Peace

Next the Universal side...

Universal
Need

Result

Physical Dispersement

Bridge

Spiritual Internalization

Now

Stepping Stones

Now:
  Stepping Stones: Productive movement.
Bridge:
  Spiritual Internalization: True identity.
Result:
  Physical Dispersement: The remote view.

We interpreted this as - We're taking the right steps. Keep it up, what we're doing is good and it will be published.

Here, the universal and human sides more or less agree. All that is needed is to do the work. The timing looks good for starting the process now.

The Three Card Spread
Affirmations that Manifest

The three card spread works wonderfully if, when things seem a bit mushy, you need a push in the right direction. It does this by creating an affirmation that will help bring resolution to an issue you are facing, or to help bring something needed into manifestation. At the very least, the three card spread will take you to the next step in your growth process.

On the surface the three card spread seems simplistic. Our experience has shown that this simplicity is only on the surface and that this is one of the most powerful spreads we have encountered. This is because the affirmation created will help take you in the direction needed, whatever that step may be.

However, there is a built in safety valve that helps keep things from moving too fast. This safety valve is called your free will choice. Your choice can say 'This is something I don't want now,' in which case the affirmation probably won't work. More importantly, stated or not, if you don't really want it in your life, the process of manifestation proceeds so slowly that you have plenty of time to allow the process to continue or to abort it.

So, prepare your question or statement carefully. Make sure that you want the results and are willing to live with the outcome. Let the three card spread be a tool that helps quickly bring your life into balanced alignment. Think about what you really want.

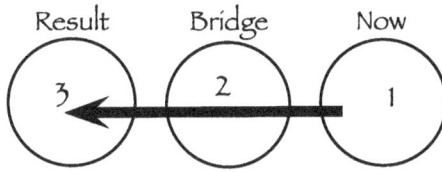

The cards are laid out in the order shown. Interpret the cards right to left starting with the now and then moving to the result. The middle card is the bridge that shows how to get from the now to the result.

After the spread is interpreted create an affirmation using the spiritual meaning of the cards. This process is best shown through an example.

The question was:
What is the best way to get the divination book published?
And the answer was:

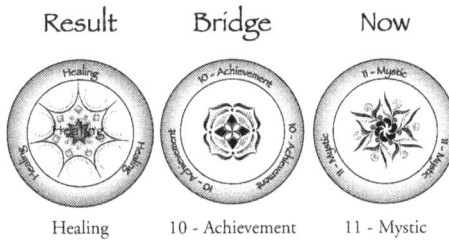

Healing   10 - Achievement   11 - Mystic

The meaning of the three cards are:

Now: 11 - Mystic: Penetrate the veil.
Bridge: 10 - Achievement: Accept potential
Result: Healing: Wellness.

A short summary would be: Looking at the hidden to bring healing through the acceptance of my potential.

Apparently the publishing of the book has a lot to do with self confidence. Well, what else is new!

Next an affirmation needs to be created using the spiritual meanings of the cards.

Now: Mystic - I am all seeing and I know.
Bridge: Achievement - I am creation and I create.
Result: Healing - I am healed

The first cut of the affirmation is:
I am healed by taking what I see and know and using that for creation.
A more cohesive affirmation might be:
I *create from what I already know and I am healed.*
Or:
I am healed by knowing that I have everything I need to create.

After using this affirmation for a bit we came to a positive understanding that, even though the book had many new concepts, it would be useful. This gave us the confidence to proceed with the publishing. In addition, we realized that it is now easier to bring hidden knowledge (The Mystic) into some useful creation.

Divination

Summary of the Cards

The 12 Foundation Energies
The ingredients

The Directions
The four perspectives.
North: The wise overview.
   I step back and I view everything that is needed.
South: The innocent details.
   I see all I need without reservation.
West: The active movement.
   I move forward in courage and faith.
East: The final form.
   I am fulfilled by what I have accomplished.

The Elements
The four ingredients.
Air: The space.
   I have the Space for all that is important to me.
Fire: The movement.
   I move forward with what I value.
Water: Gather together.
   I create by shaping what is around me.
Earth: The solidity.
   I have already what is needed in my life.

The Winds
The four movements.
North Wind: The pause to assimilate.
   I accept now that I am complete.
South Wind: Active learning.
   I already have all knowledge needed.
West Wind: Stimulation.
   I am the courage to leap into the unknown.
East Wind: Finishing.
   I am poised and ready for the step into my future.

The 12 Wisdom Energies
The twelve arenas

12 - New Beginnings: The dawning of newness.
> I am ready to create newness without reservation.

1 - Subconscious: Information surfaces.
> I know that I know all that I need to know.

2 - Merger: Bringing together.
> I open my mind to new partnerships and new creation

3 - Foundations: Basis for understanding.
> I already have all knowledge for complete use of my potential.

4 - Elevated View: Seeking greater meaning.
> I release all preconceived concepts and allow wisdom to surface.

5 - Instigation: Push to get started.
> Without reservation, I take the next step.

6. - Manifestation: Bring nebulous into form.
> I am ready to accept the resolution.

7 - Truth in Movement: Changing truth.
> I am freed from past perspective and find a new truth.

8 - Opposite's: The other side.
> I am ready to observe and even become the other perspective.

9 - Expansion: Productive growth.
> I have no limit that binds me to the past.

10 - Achievement: Accept potential.
> I am creation and I create.

11 - Mystic: Penetrate the veil.
> I am all seeing and I know.

Divination

The 12 Laniscate Energies
The steps of manifestation

1 - Dawning: Life is present.
   I am the Universe through everything that is around me.

2 - Awakening: Stirring of life.
   I am aware and I have potential.

3 - Greeting: Recognize life.
   I greet my potential.

4. - Asking: Action toward movement.
   I give myself permission to release my potential.

5 - Reflection: Response to movement.
   I qualify and accept my identity and my uniqueness.

6 - Launching: Decision to manifest.
   Without reservation, I step forth.

7 - Release and Acceptance: Release concepts.
   I release all that holds me from my greatest accomplishment.

8 - Energy of Manifestation: Universal response.
   I step forward with my acceptance of my power to manifest.

9 - Foundation: Ingredients of manifesting.
   I gather around me all that I need for my greatest manifestation.

10 - Beginnings: Movement of manifestation.
   I move forward to manifesting what I need.

11 - Manifestation: Act of manifesting.
   I bring into manifestation what I need.

12 - Solidification: Result of manifestation.
   I am fulfilled by what I have manifested.

The 12 Receptacles
The holders of energy

Internalization - The Apparent Facts.
  Physical: The look.
     I am that I am.
  Mental: Values.
     I recognize what I value.
  Spiritual: True identity.
     I am one with my purpose.
Integration - The Facts Harmonize.
  Spiritual: Environmental identity.
     I am one with my environment.
  Mental: Perception vs need.
     I allow my uniqueness to create.
  Physical: Pathways.
     I am fulfilled by who I am.
Interaction - The Facts Influenced.
  Physical: Movement to awareness.
     I communicate that which is mine through my acceptance of myself.
  Mental: Communicate understanding.
     My values are not tempered by the opinion of others.
  Spiritual: Purpose.
     I communicate what I know and I know what I communicate.
Dispersement - The Facts Shared.
  Spiritual: Identity.
     I send what I value into the Universe and I receive in return acceptance.
  Mental: Perceive.
     I express my greatest wisdom in service to everything that is around me.
  Physical: The remote view.
     I project my identity and receive understanding in return.

Divination

The Witness Energies
The bridges

Manifestation: What is needed.
   I manifest.
Healing: Wellness.
   I am healed.
Questions: Clarity.
   I have the answer within me.
Introspection: The Space for truth.
   I see, from my deepest self, who I am.
Communication: Bridge through interaction.
   I give and I receive at all levels.
Rejuvenation: Rebuilding.
   I am transformed and I accept the transformation.
Peace: Hold off chaos.
   I am peace.

The Growth Energies
The journey

Inward Funnel: Outside-in renewal.
   I step back into my own self and I am rejuvenated.
Outward Funnel: Inside-out regeneration.
   I transform all within me to unequivocal acceptance of
   who I am.
Stepping Stones: Productive movement.
   I joyously take the next step.
Seed: The new germ.
   I am the seed from which all grows.
Bridge: Spanning the unknown.
   I courageously look at, and then step into the unknown.

Part V The Details of the Energies

The Foundation Energies
NORTH

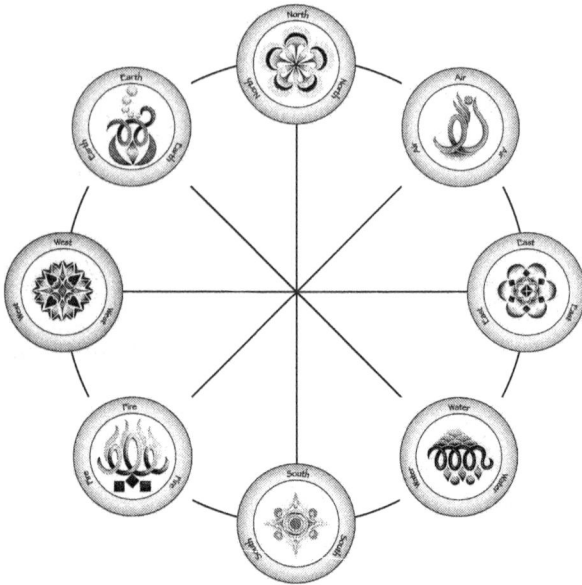

These eight energies are always present even if they are not recognized. Every time you have the simplest thought or build the most complex project the Foundation Energies are present and are at work.

The North gives an overview of what needs to be manifested. South gives you the details of everything and anything that is needed in order to manifest. West gets you up and moving along the steps of creation. East allows you to see and use the final stable form. Air creates a Space that allows the movement of Fire to enter. Water takes the movement and condenses it into something that can be shaped. Earth takes what can be shaped and solidifies it. Additionally, the Winds provide the force needed to bring everything into manifestation.

What follows is a more detailed description of the Foundation Energies.

Energy Details

The Directions

The directions provide the perspective needed to see and to understand what is to be manifested.

North
The wise overview.

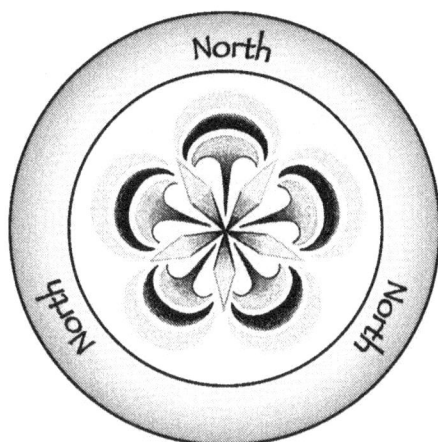

Mental: North is the energy that allows you to see the forest without the need to see the trees. It brings into focus the overall view, not the details. It is as if you are above the topic and looking down upon it. North brings everything that surrounds and is connected to the topic into view. It is the energy of clarity from an overview perspective. North's perspective comes from pure wisdom. It is a free will choice to use its perspective wisely.

Physical: From a personal perspective, North shows a need to get away from the details, step back and take a new look. It's time to follow a new path that has less resistance.

Spiritual: I step back and I view everything that is needed.

South
The innocent details.

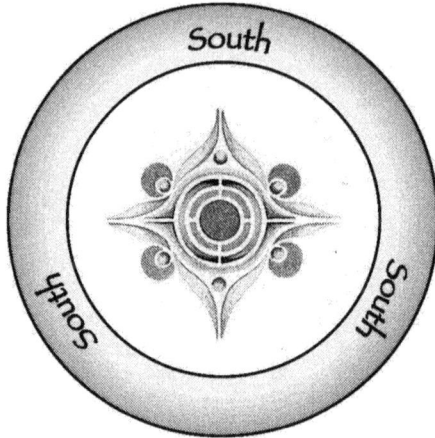

Mental: The perspective of South is peripheral in nature. It is the view of the trees, not the forest. It is a 360° view. You can stand in the center and look all around you without the need to turn your head. If more detail is needed, South allows you to focus on whatever level of detail you need in order to obtain the information necessary. South shows you all the components of whatever you need to examine from an underlying perspective of innocence.

Physical: The personal perspective of South shows a need to look at what is needed in order to progress with your issue or project. It is time to move forward, but also time to look at what you are getting into. Evaluate with the perspective of moving on.

Spiritual: I see all I need without reservation.

Energy Details

West

The active movement.

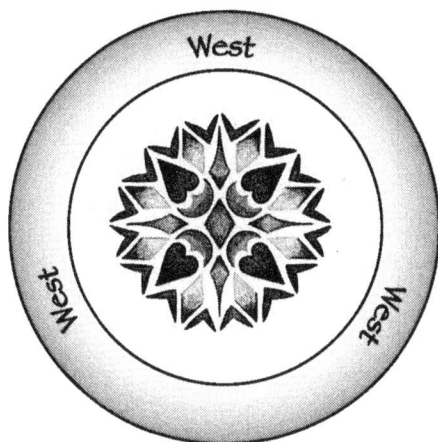

Mental: West is an instigative energy that says "let's get going on the project." West also allows you to see the best way to proceed with the project, and it provides the energy that works toward completion. All the steps necessary to work on a project, be the project examining an emotional issue or building a house, are seen with the aid of the West.

Physical: The personal perspective of West is to get off your duff and get going. Everything needed is at hand and procrastination no longer will work. It is time to start, or to make a conscious decision to not do it.

Spiritual: I move forward in courage and faith.

East

The final form.

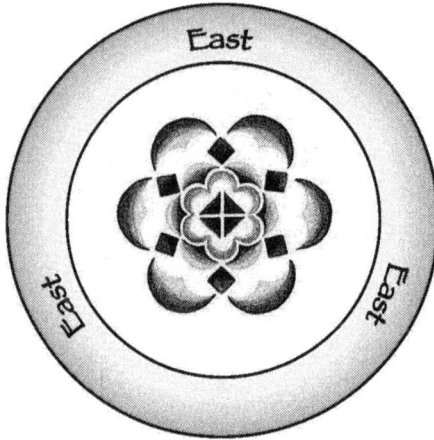

Mental: East is the energy of completion. It allows the final form of a physical project to be seen, or the resolution of an issue to be formed. It is also the energy of maintenance that binds together whatever has been created. If it weren't for East, the chair you just built would collapse, or the balance just brought into an issue would instantly disappear. East provides the perception that glues together everything into its final form.

Physical: The personal perspective of East is satisfaction with what you have accomplished. It is time to stop fine tuning and to get on with the next project or issue. Pat yourself on the back for what has been accomplished and get on with life.

Spiritual: I am fulfilled by what I have accomplished.

Energy Details

The Elements

The ingredients needed for manifestation.

*A*ir

Creation of the space.

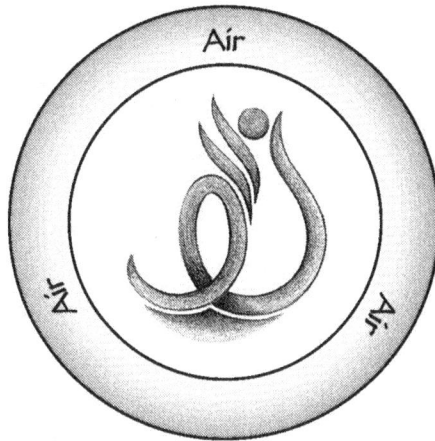

Mental: The lightest of the elements, Air, is the energy which opens a Space that allows manifestation to occur. It is an expansive energy. In its etheric form it has no movement, just the ability to create an arena allowing everything else to occur. Air is represented by the heart chakra and, as such, brings in the ability to touch and be touched. Air creates the Space to bring things in and to allow whatever is brought in to be used. It doesn't do the bringing in and using part, it just creates the Space for manifestation to occur. When you establish Air you create space.

Physical: From a personal perspective, Air shows a need to create a new arena or Space for new ideas and points-of-view. Take your present position and let it expand into something that is new.

Spiritual: I have the Space for all that is important to me.

Fire
Creation of movement.

Mental: The active movement of Fire brings everything that is needed for manifestation into the arena that was created by air. It is a fast movement that has the ability to mix and stir. Fire is represented by the solar plexus chakra and thereby has the ability, through insight, to see the real purpose of the manifestation. The impersonal energy of Fire always brings in the appropriate ingredients to manifest whatever is called for. The energies brought in are still not ready for manifestation, but they are in movement and ready to be used.

Physical: The personal perspective of Fire is movement. It is time to stir the pot and bring in new ingredients for old ideas. It's time to shake things up and go on.

Spiritual: I move forward with what I value.

Energy Details

Water
Contraction.

Mental: Water takes that which is in movement and condenses it into a shapable form. It takes what has been brought in and moved by Fire, and consolidates it into something that is ready to be made solid. Water does not make it solid, but it does give it the fluidity necessary to be shaped into solidity. Water is represented by the sacral chakra and therefore brings in the ability to create.

Physical: From a personal perception Water says that it is time to make use of what you have. Things are ready to be taken to a new level and used in a new way. There is light at the end of the tunnel, and you can see it if you look.

Spiritual: I create by shaping what is around me.

Earth
Creation of the solidity.

Mental: Earth takes what is shapable and brings it to its final physical form. Then it provides the energy necessary to maintain the final form. Earth doesn't care if the final form is a thought, an attitude or a solid object. It simply brings it into a form that can be felt or touched mentally, emotionally or physically. Earth is represented by the root chakra, and as such provides the vital force to keep things alive, be it of the mind or of the physical world.

Physical: The personal perspective of Earth is one of fulfillment. It is time to see your creation's value and to feel good about it. Take what you have and give it the love and caring necessary for it to be recognized and used.

Spiritual: I have already what is needed in my life.

Energy Details

The Four Winds

The movements needed for manifestation.

North Wind
The pause to assimilate.

Mental: The direction north represents the overview perspective. As a result of a clear understanding of what needs to be accomplished, the North Wind, or the movement of the North perspective, provides the impetus to reflect upon what needs to be done. The North Wind is active reflection upon what is to be accomplished. It is a pause that allows the act of manifestation to proceed or be aborted.

Physical: The personal perspective of the North Wind is basically a pilgrimage. It strongly suggests that you get away from the mundane in order to gain a new, clearer point of view. This doesn't necessarily mean a physical trip but it does imply that a time out is needed away from the hustle bustle of your normal life. An hour, a day, or an extended vacation is needed. Use the time to reflect back upon your life and what you truly value.

Spiritual: I accept now that I am complete.

South Wind
Active & innocent learning.

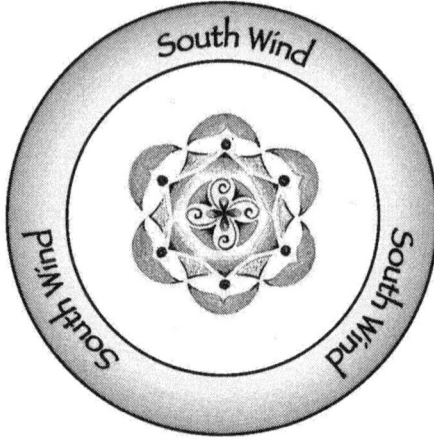

Mental: The direction south gives the detail perspective. The movement of that perspective is the South Wind which brings active research into what needs to be accomplished. The research does not involve libraries, etc. It is instantaneous and subconscious, and involves only what has been individually assimilated through experience but without the burden of negativity. The South Wind's innocence allows a fresh start in any process that builds toward manifestation, independently of the amount of work needed.

Physical: The personal perspective of the South Wind is to actively pursue the collection of all facts, issues and details concerning the project or question you are working on. It is time to take action through research and planning. Consider all details and possibilities.

Spiritual: I already have all knowledge needed.

Energy Details

West Wind

Stimulation toward movement.

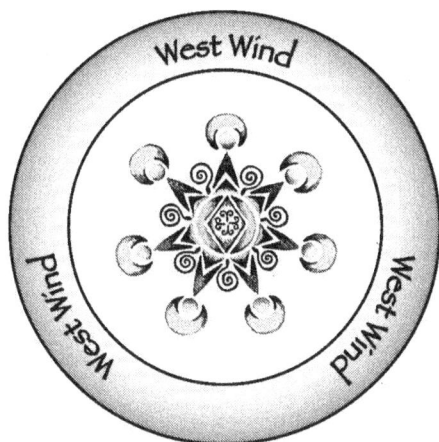

Mental: The west provides the courageous thrust that leads to all the work needed to manifest. The West Wind provides the energy needed in order to accomplish the work. In addition, by creating a wave of courage, the West Wind brings the determination needed to finish the work. Through the West Wind's impetus, courage and determination are created that can lead to successful completion of any work.

Physical: From a personal perspective the West Wind is saying go for it. It's now time to get off your duff and get to work. Everything is aligned for a successful completion. Nothing stands in your way save a lack of courage or commitment.

Spiritual: I am the courage to leap into the unknown.

East Wind

An awakening about the future.

Mental: The direction east is the perspective of completion and the maintenance of what has manifested. The East Wind takes that which has been manifested and readies it for the next step, whatever that may be. The East Wind creates an uneasiness that says there is something that needs to be accomplished. It is the energy that guards against complacency. It is a gentle movement that says OK, now that it has been accomplished, what is next?

Physical: The personal perspective of the East Wind is completion. It's time to wrap things up and get on with whatever is next in store for you. This does not mean complete release of your project, for there is still nurturing needed. However, it is time to acknowledge that the work is complete.

Spiritual: I am poised and ready for the step into my future.

Energy Details

The Wisdom Energies

The wisdom cards are made up of twelve unique energies that represent twelve different arenas that, in turn bring clarity to any type of interaction.

The twelve energies of the Wisdom Circle are New Beginnings, Subconscious, Merger, Foundation, Elevated View, Instigation, Manifestation, Truth in Movement, Opposite's, Expansion, Achievement and the Mystic.

The Wisdom Circle is laid out as depicted below:

NORTH

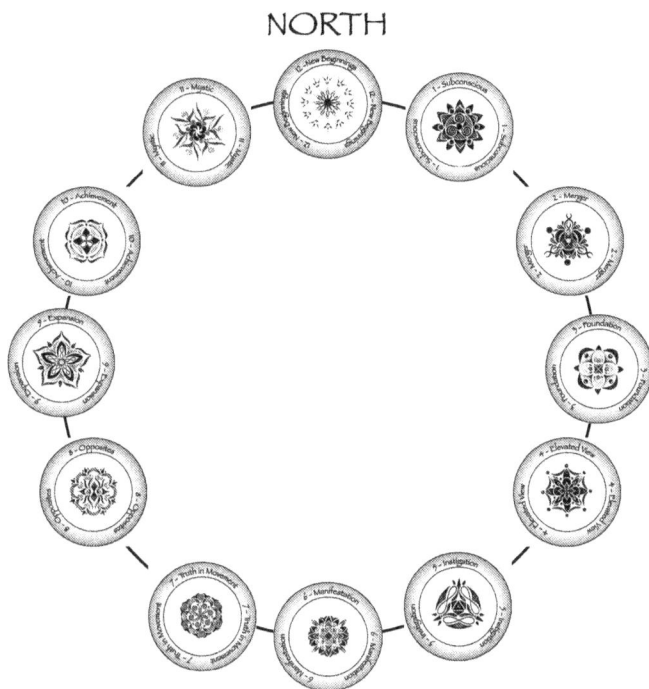

These are pure energies and not their physical representation. For instance, the mystic represents the energy that is mystical, not the person who is the mystic, or for that matter, who uses the mystic energy. In other words, each of the twelve energies represents a unique aspect of pure Universal consciousness.

The Wisdom Energies create clarity via movement of Universal energy in a manner that allows the energy to be physically or emotionally felt. They modulate Universal energy in a way that identifies both the obvious and hidden purpose of the question. The information presented is understandable by and related to the person who is in need of the results. The Wisdom Energies are direct and wisely guide you along your path of development.

What follows is a detailed description of the twelve Wisdom Energies depicted by the cards. As you go over these energies remember that they represent arenas which create a Space to bring wisdom into any question, issue or stated purpose. They create an attitude or Space that can give birth to the answer. The Space is mental in nature, so with a bit of practice, the wisdom cards can become a source of spiritual insight to aid in any aspect of growth.

Energy Details

12 - New Beginnings

The dawning of newness

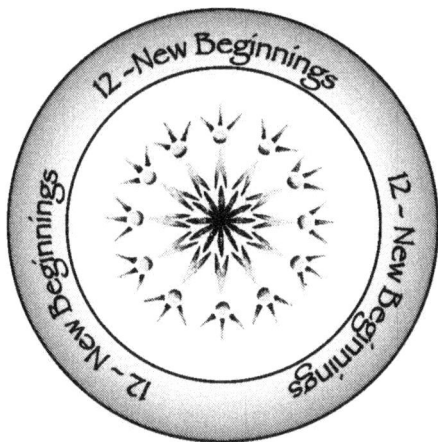

Mental: The energy of New Beginnings is a dawning energy of anything that is different from what was previously known. It is the symbolic light bulb, turning on when a new concept is discovered. It is not the start of a new project, but rather the energy of discovery that gives rise to the new project.

Physical: This energy, on a personal level, indicates that not only are new concepts needed but also that a new concept is before you. Absorb the quiet joy that comes from knowing that there is something better that can be discovered. The courage it takes to accept the new is yours. Move with it into the future.

Spiritual: I am ready to create newness without reservation.

1 - Subconscious
Hidden Within

Mental: The energy of the Subconscious is that which lies hidden within your mind. It is the latent knowing that something needs to be brought to the surface for examination. It can be old information that needs to be re-used or that which you didn't know existed. The Subconscious is the memory bank that holds all your experiences, including some from past lives.

Physical: This energy, on a personal level, means that you have hidden information that is ready to come to the surface. Know that the information is there to help you better understand whatever process you are going through. It is to eliminate pain - not to cause it.

Spiritual: I know that I know all that I need to know.

Energy Details

2 - *Merger*
Bringing Together

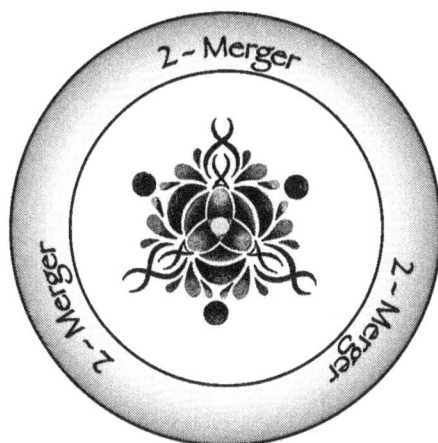

Mental: The energy of Merger allows two to become one. It can be two different ideas or perceptions, or even dissimilar attitudes. This is not the energy of compromise; it is the energy of elevated thought that allows commonality to be seen. Balance is achieved when the highest form of two perceptions merge.

Physical: This energy, on a personal level, means that it is time to bring together that which you thought didn't belong together. The first step of healing, or for that matter, manifestation, is to recognize commonality between purpose and end result. The Energy of Merger will provide the acceptance of that commonality

Spiritual: I open my mind to new partnerships and new creation.

3 - Foundation
Basis for Understanding

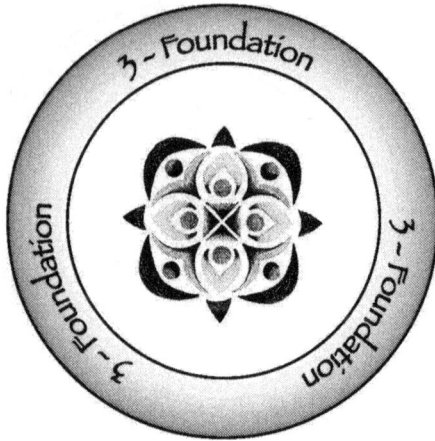

Mental: The energy of Foundation is that which provides a basis to bring new from the old. It can be the ingredients for manifestation, or the comfort that is felt after a good decision is made. It is what gives the feeling that you are standing on solid ground and have whatever is needed to build new from old. It is a nurturing energy that you can recall if things become uncertain.

Physical: This energy, on a personal level, means that you are ready and able to begin a new project. Everything that you need is within your grasp. This energy sustains you in uncertain times and builds the dedication needed to bring about completion.

Spiritual: I already have all knowledge for complete use of my potential.

Energy Details

4 - Elevated View
Seeking the Greater Meaning

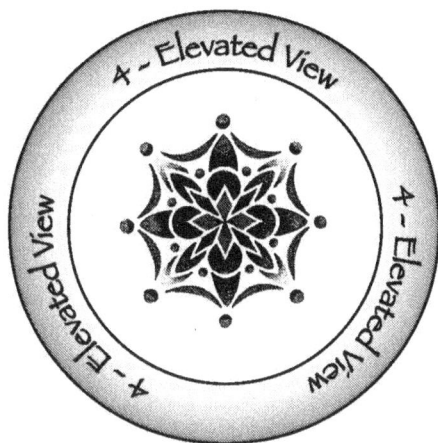

Mental: The energy of Elevated View brings about a mental attitude that allows the entire picture to be seen. It provides a view that is beyond logic and it taps into the superconscious mind. It takes you to a perspective that is beyond ego, yet it allows the practical side to be seen. The energy of Elevated View bridges spirit and matter in a way that is useful.

Physical: This energy, on a personal level, means that it is time to release old concepts. You are ready to see the true picture and have the means to apply it in your daily life. The energy of Elevated View brings a joy that transcends human feelings, yet it does not remove you from daily tasks.

Spiritual: I release all preconceived concepts and allow wisdom to surface.

5 - *Instigation*
The Push to Get Started

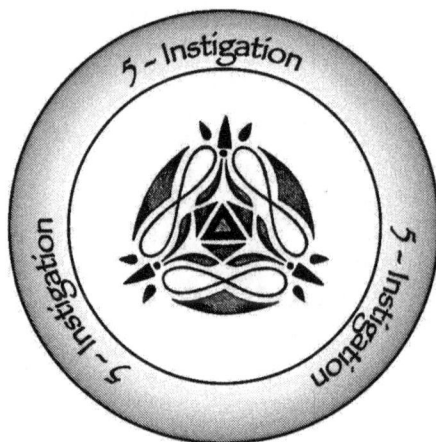

Mental: The energy of Instigation says there is something to be done, and this is the time to get started. It is a push that makes you get off your duff and get going. It is not the energy of movement, rather it is the push behind the movement. The energy of Instigation prepares you for whatever is needed to get on with life. It also creates a clear Space that allows courage and faith to be found.

Physical: This energy, on a personal level, says that it is time for movement. You still need to provide the initiative that gets you started, but the timing is now. Your free will choice will determine whether or not you get going. Even though this is an active energy, it provides a gentle push, rather than a demand that you must do anything.

Spiritual: Without reservation, I take the next step.

Energy Details

6 - Manifestation
Bringing Nebulous Into Form

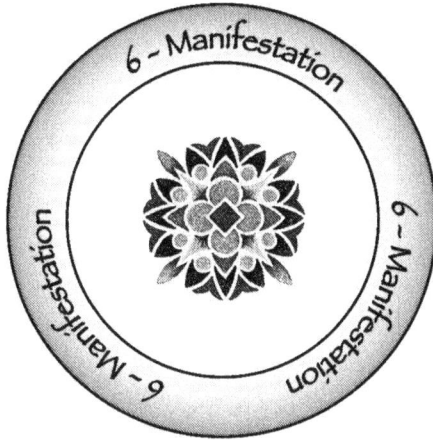

Mental: The energy of Manifestation is an anchoring energy that sustains a thought or project through to completion. It is not the energy of work, but it does provide the sustaining energy that allows work to be accomplished. It maintains the focus necessary to bring creative movement to completion.

Physical: The energy of Manifestation, on a personal level, means that projects are ready to be wrapped up or issues are ready for resolution. It is not time to abandon the project; rather it is time to bring it to resolution. Everything is in order for completion and only your action is required. It is time to stop thinking about it and just do it.

Spiritual: I am ready to accept the resolution.

7 - *Truth in Movement*
Truth Changes

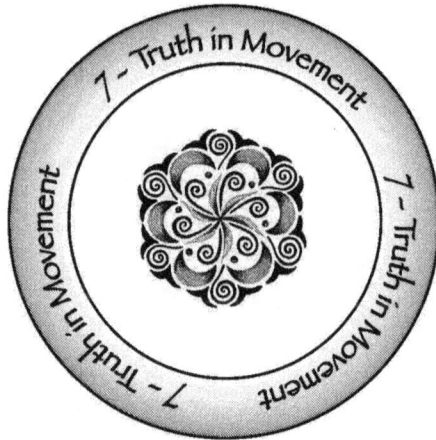

Mental: The energy of Truth in Movement is the energy that allows opinions to change. It isn't the new opinion itself, but it does provide a new look at an old issue. This is an energy which creates an arena for new perspectives such that stagnation can be broken. It is an energy that allows old perspectives to mold into new ideas.

Physical: The energy of Truth in Movement, on a personal level, means that old concepts are no longer serving you. It is time for opinions to change. It is time to be open to new ideas and to put the past behind you. Don't worry about the ramifications of change. Truth comes from the superconscious mind and the superconscious always knows what's best.

Spiritual: I am freed from past perspective and find a new truth.

Energy Details

8 - *Opposite's*
The Other Side

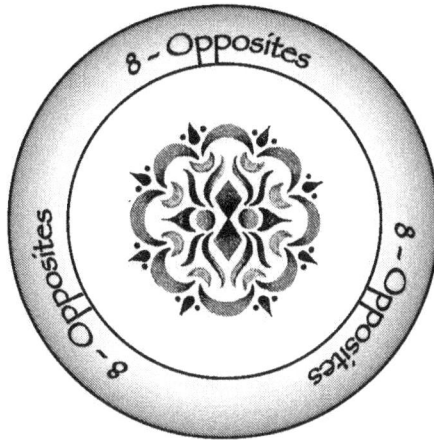

Mental: The energy of Opposite's is an energy that allows the other side to be seen. It does not manifest the opposite, but it does provide the energy necessary to see and accept the other side. It is through polarities that balance can be achieved. This is an energy that works with all polarities, be they between the spiritual world and the physical world or between two opposite beliefs.

Physical: The energy of Opposites, on a personal level, means that both sides of an issue need to be looked at. Following the current line of thought is not productive. The time is appropriate for the other perspective to be seen. However, following another perspective is a free will choice. If the old perspective was not productive, change is needed.

Spiritual: I am ready to observe and even become the other perspective.

9 - *Expansion*
Productive Growth

Mental: The energy of Expansion takes the current condition beyond its known potential. A new Space is created that allows a greater potential to be seen. Expansion provides the attitude necessary to bring new ideas and perspectives into focus. It doesn't throw away the old, but it does provide an energy that can move the old forward into new potential and perspective. The past gives way to an expanded future. With the acceptance of Expansion anything can come into manifestation.

Physical: The energy of Expansion, on a personal level, means that it is time to put old concepts behind you. It is time for the old to be allowed to grow into something that will better serve you in the present and in the unfolding future. Even those things that are serving you well can expand into something that serves even better. It is time to let go and look at the future.

Spiritual: I have no limit that binds me to the past.

Energy Details

10 - Achievement
Acceptance of Potential

Mental: The energy of Achievement creates an energy that can bring nebulous concepts into a form which can be touched mentally or physically. It is an energy that allows you to see what is needed for the creative thrust to occur. The energy of Achievement also forms an arena that allows the unknown to be penetrated.

Physical: The energy of Achievement, on a personal level, signals you that it is time to create, even if you aren't sure how to get started. It is time to let the Universe show you the way. Let confidence grow from uncertainty and bring greater happiness and prosperity into your life. As it was with the ancient alchemists, the ingredients to manifest what you want and need come from the most unsuspected places. Be open and let the new into your life.

Spiritual: I am creation and I create.

11 - Mystic
Penetration of the Veil

Mental: The energy of the Mystic creates a Space for the magician to emerge. It is not the physical magician, but it is the energy of the magician. It allows you to see through the foggy veil into a Space that provides clear insight. The mystical Space knows no boundaries, only that which must be seen in order to be taken to a more practical and useful level. The mystical lens lets you see into the heart of the matter without fear.

Physical: The energy of the Mystic, on a personal level, means that it is time to see and experience that which was heretofore unknown. It is time to bring greater clarity into your life. That which you used to fear no longer needs to hold a power over you.

Spiritual: I am all seeing and I know.

The Laniscate Energies

The geometric form of the Laniscate represents a movement of energy that holds and relates to the act of manifestation. Every Laniscate has twelve energies that represent twelve steps of manifestation. The Laniscate's energy flows in a receptive or counter clockwise direction in the South. The energy movement continues in a clockwise or active direction in the North loop.

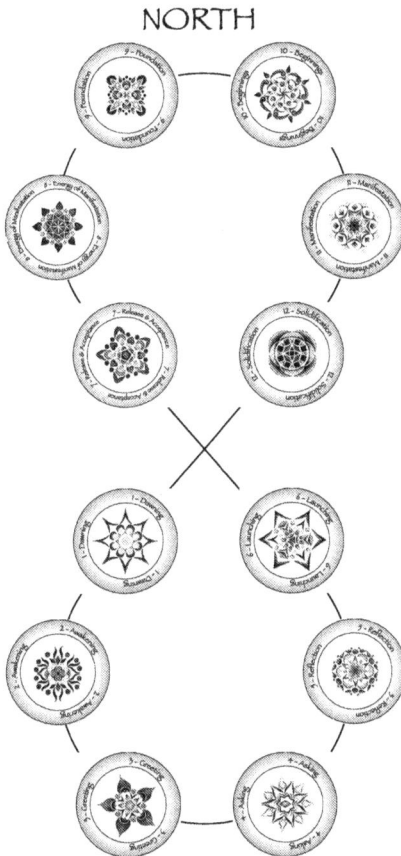

NORTH

The manifestation path starts by passing through the energies of Dawning, Awakening, Greeting, Asking, Reflection and Launching. The receptive direction of that loop means that the first six stages of manifestation bring about a clarity in that which is to be manifested. The second loop of the Laniscate passes through the energies of Release and Acceptance, Energy of Manifestation, Foundation, Beginnings, Manifestation and Solidification. The active direction of that loop brings manifestation into a touchable form.

What follows is a detailed description of the Laniscate Energies.

1 - Dawning

Mental: The energy of Dawning is the quiescent energy that exists at sunrise. There is no movement either physically or mentally. It is a state of being, of being one with yourself yet contained within the Universe.

Physical: The personal meaning of Dawning is to let go of movement and escape into your inner-most being. It is time to escape from the complexities of existence for a moment and be one with the Universe.

Spiritual: I am the Universe through everything that is around me.

Energy Details

2 - Awakening

Mental: The energy of Awakening is the first stirring of life and thought. It is not an active energy or movement. It is that moment when there is a recognition of life and that you are alive. Awakening creates an arena that allows you to recognize purpose in your existence, while there is still no need to react to purpose or to take action.

Physical: From a personal perspective, Awakening tells you that there is a need to be aware of the potential that rests within you. It is not yet time to react, but it is time to awaken the potential that is part of your soul. It is felt deeply, yet without the need to react.

Spiritual: I am aware and I have potential.

3 - Greeting

Mental: The energy of Greeting is a recognition of life. It says that there is life around you that supports you, and it needs to be acknowledged. It is the hello or handshake that occurs when friends meet. The Sanskrit word 'namaste' describes the greeting, "The God in me greets the God in you and together we are one." Greeting creates a oneness between you and all things. The oneness created has no pecking order. All things are equal.

Physical: From a personal perspective, Greeting says to let go of ego and look around you for help or influence. It is time to prepare to move forward into an attitude of equality. It is time to be friends with yourself.

Spiritual: I greet my potential.

Energy Details

4 - Asking

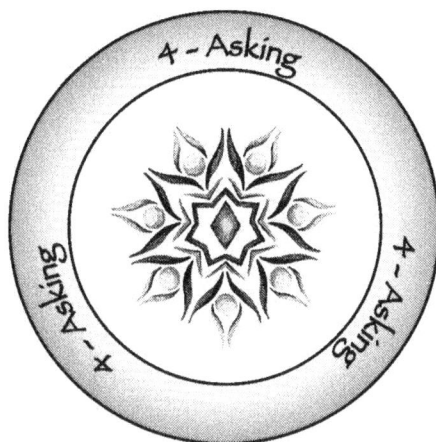

Mental: The energy of Asking is the first movement toward action. Asking says, "Is it time for me to move forward?" And the answer is always yes. It is the interaction that gives permission to proceed.

Physical: From a personal level, Asking means that it is time to make a decision. Proceeding onward is a free-will choice, but the Universe is ready for movement, and it is up to you to go forward.

Spiritual: I give myself permission to release my potential.

5 - Reflection

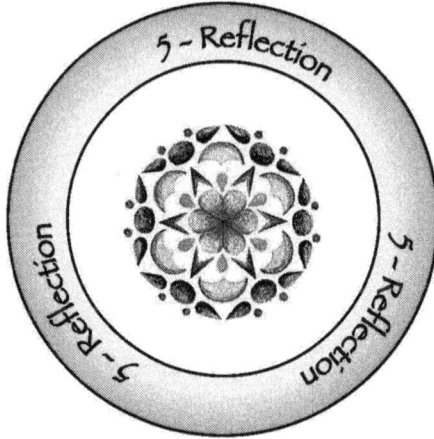

Mental: The energy of Reflection is a response to the first movement. It is the energy that allows integration of the decision for movement to take place. It is an inward movement that creates a basis for movement to occur.

Physical: From a personal perspective. Reflection gives you the Space to become comfortable with your decision. It also gives you the opportunity to fine tune your decision. Be comfortable with yourself and your decisions. This is an opportunity to modify whatever needs to be accomplished.

Spiritual: I qualify and accept my identity and my uniqueness.

Energy Details

6 - Launching

Mental: The energy of Launching creates a decision to manifest. It is a point of no return from the implementation of any decision you make. If the decision needs to be modified or reversed, that decision is made later. It is the energy of action, and action happens.

Physical: From a personal perspective, Launching gives you the blind courage to proceed with your plan. It places you in a perspective where uncertainty does not exist. You are ready for action and action begins.

Spiritual: Without reservation, I step forth.

7 - Release and Acceptance

Mental: The energy of Release and Acceptance removes any preconceived notions about how manifestation will occur. It allows an internal knowing that manifestation is possible. Old concepts are out the window and new concepts are accepted.

Physical: From a personal perspective, Release and Acceptance means that it is time to release your current concept as to how things should go and to accept that it will turn out for the best. The old gives way to the new and you have the courage to proceed.

Spiritual: I release all that holds me from my greatest accomplishment.

8 - Energy of Manifestation

Mental: Energy of Manifestation is a Universal response to the acceptance of manifestation. It is not the step or process of manifestation, it is the energy that allows manifestation to occur. Manifestation is ready to occur, but it is still not in movement. The potential to manifest is present and ready to proceed.

Physical: From a personal perspective, Energy of Manifestation says to take the next step. Do not hesitate because everything you need to complete your goal is present. Go ahead.

Spiritual: I step forward with my acceptance of my power to manifest.

9 - Foundation

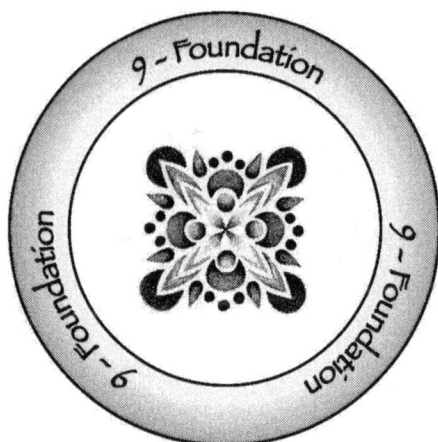

Mental: The energy of Foundation brings the ingredients of manifestation into the process of manifestation. The ingredients are not mixed or put together in their final manifest form yet, but everything is in place and manifestation is ready.

Physical: From a personal perspective, the Foundation energy means continue your current path. Don't look back; everything will come together as you need it.

Spiritual: I gather around me all that I need for my greatest manifestation.

Energy Details

10 - Beginnings

Mental: The energy of Beginnings is the movement of the ingredients of manifestation. Manifestation is eminent. The process of manifestation begins and will result from what has been set in motion.

Physical: From a personal perspective, Beginnings means that it is too late to turn back. The wheels are in motion, and the results will bring what is needed. Relax and observe.

Spiritual: I move forward to manifesting what I need.

11 - Manifestation

Mental: The energy of Manifestation is the act of manifesting. The ingredients are coming together, and the final form is being produced. The Universe is now in charge, and it knows how to complete the process.

Physical: From a personal perceptive, Manifestation means it is time to get out of the way and to let it happen. Let go of the outcome. Keep your intent alive, and let the Universe guide you.

Spiritual: I bring into manifestation what I need.

12 - Solidification

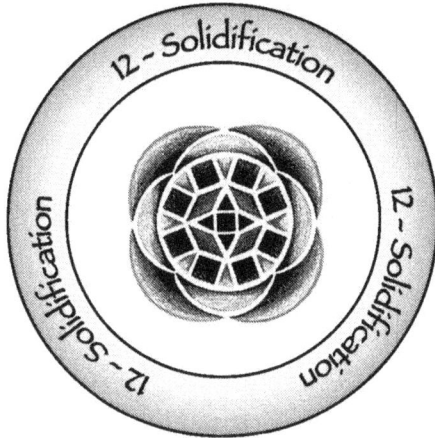

Mental: The energy of Solidification is the result of mani-festation. It is the final form and is no longer malleable by thought or deed. Solidification is a fulfilling energy for a job well done. The Universe is in balance.

Physical: From a personal perspective, Solidification says step back and observe what you have created. It does not have a personality that says that it is good or bad. It is done. Now, what are you going to do about it? There are no mistakes, only growth. Take what you have and use it as best you can. Feel the fulfillment of accomplishment.

Spiritual: I am fulfilled by what I have manifested.

The Receptacle Energies

Every question or issue relates to a present state of being that contains twelve receptacles that hold the attitudes and facts associated with that state of being. The receptacles are a holding area that keeps the purpose of the interaction alive until a new state of being (understanding) is achieved.

Each receptacle is contained in a quadrant that gives the receptacle a more focused purpose. The receptacles are arranged as follows:

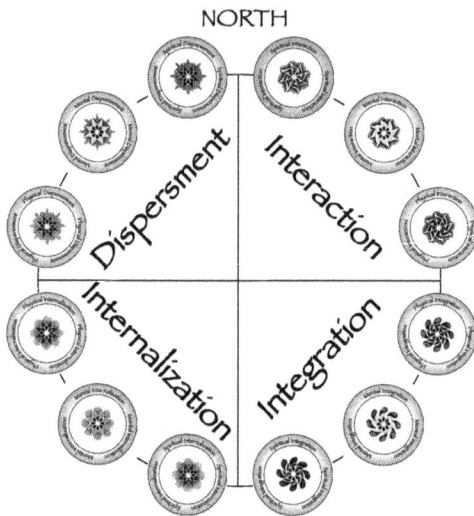

The receptacle energies are a great help for holding the emotional attitudes at arm's length, so-to-speak, so they can be viewed without bias. They also provide a mixing area to bring all parts of an issue or question together for resolution.

The Quadrant of Internalization
The Apparent Fact

Physical Internalization

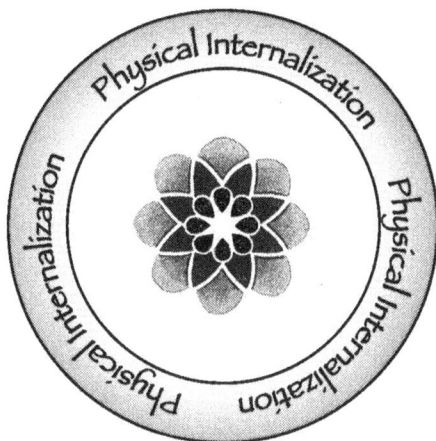

Mental: The way the site presents itself from the outside in, so-to-speak. This receptacle is what contains the physical look of the site and therefore how the site is seen by those who physically visit and use it.

Physical: From a personal perspective, the Receptacle of Physical Internalization has to do with the way you view yourself. It means that it is necessary for you to take a good look at yourself and determine if what you see meets with your approval. Take a look in the mirror and either accept what you see or make a decision to change. This can mean a simple change in wardrobe or hair style. Or it can signal the start of a complete attitude makeover. It is time to bring what you see about yourself into balance.

Spiritual: I am that I am.

Mental Internalization

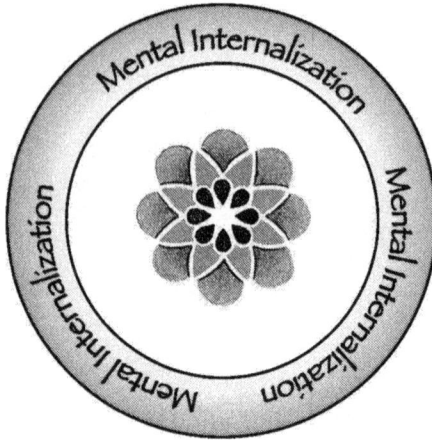

Mental: This receptacle holds what the site values, or what is important in order to maintain the site's inner identity. Its inner identity is the purpose behind the site's birth or dedication. This purpose evolves as time and perception evolve.

Physical: From a personal perspective, the Receptacle of Mental Internalization says pay attention to what you value. It signals that it is time to take a good look at what you value and re-evaluate or change it so it can expand. In any event, this receptacle says things need a new perspective. Re-evaluate and single mindfully move on.

Spiritual: I recognize what I value.

Spiritual Internalization

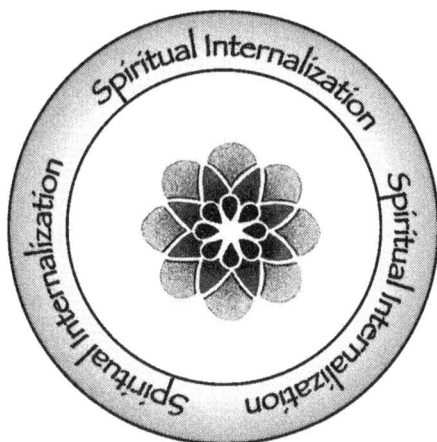

Mental: This receptacle holds the Universal identity of the site as it was defined at its birth or dedication. This is the site's true identity and holds the inner energy or the feeling of the site.

Physical: From a personal perspective, the Receptacle of Spiritual Internalization says to look at how you relate to your immediate environment. Look at yourself and know that you are unique and perfect. This is not time for an identity crisis, but for self confidence. You are uniquely qualified to accomplish whatever is needed within the confines of the environment that you have created for yourself.

Spiritual: I am one with my purpose.

The Quadrant of Integration
The Facts Harmonize

Spiritual Integration

Mental: This receptacle holds the energy that integrates the identity of the site with its environment. It holds the energy of the site's life that brings it into a homogeneous whole.

Physical: From a personal perspective, the Receptacle of Spiritual Integration has to do with your relationship to your emotional foundations. Everything around you is important because it is what you have chosen to work with concerning your spiritual growth. This includes your family as well as your home and work environments. Look around you and see what is to be accomplished. See what you have created.

Spiritual: I am one with my environment.

Energy Details

Mental Integration

Mental: This receptacle holds the merger of outside perception and the inner need of the site to express its identity. It maintains a bridge between external influences and the site's identity.

Physical: From a personal perspective, the Receptacle of Mental Integration stands for the creative expression of your energy. Your life is your creation and it is your responsibility to nurture it. If it seems like a change is needed, take a risk and be creative in your solution. Look at what you value and act accordingly.

Spiritual: I allow my uniqueness to create.

Physical Integration

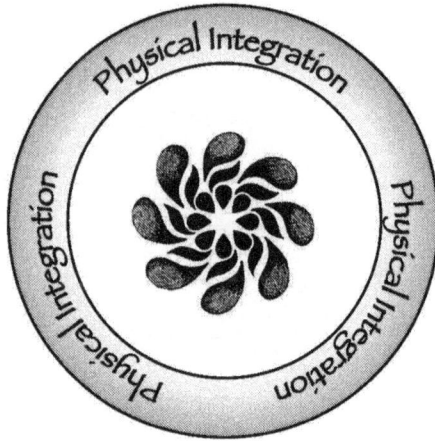

Mental: This receptacle holds the physical pathways through the site. It holds the energy to block protected regions from physical access by those who are not ready for access. It is not a protective energy but rather an energy that allows proper timing to be used.

Physical: From a personal perspective, the Receptacle of Physical Integration has to do with fulfillment. How you find fulfillment in your work and the way that you gain fulfillment through service. If the fulfillment isn't there, be prepared for physical ramifications. There is a direct link between how you physically feel and how happy you are.

Spiritual: I am fulfilled by who I am.

The Quadrant of Interaction
The Facts Influenced

Physical Interaction

Mental: This receptacle holds the energy of physical movement in and around the site. It helps temper any physical movement in a way that helps to increase awareness of the site's identity without inhibiting the curiosity of the visitor.

Physical: From a personal perspective, the Receptacle of Physical Interaction represents communication at a physical level, including verbal as well as body language. The interaction results in a physical act to be accomplished involving everything that is outside of yourself. It represents the need for interaction with another person.

Spiritual: I communicate that which is mine through my acceptance of myself.

Mental Interaction

Mental: This receptacle holds the thoughts that bridge the site's identity and the state of mind of the users of the site. This receptacle provides an understanding that allows mental interaction to occur. It bridges understanding so communication can take place.

Physical: From a personal perspective, the Receptacle of Mental Interaction represents communication about your state of mind concerning your values. This can be accomplished through verbal communication concerning your feelings or deeper attitudes. This receptacle has to do with the need to cultivate friendships with all aspects of your life and your environment.

Spiritual: My values are not tempered by the opinion of others.

Spiritual Interaction

Mental: This receptacle holds the dedicated purpose of the site and the interaction with the user's intentions. This is held in a way that does not trivialize the site's purpose or identity. This sharing of the site's identity is done in a way that is understandable by the user.

Physical: From a personal perspective, the Receptacle of Spiritual Interaction represents all forms of communication that lead to greater understanding. This means listening as well as speaking. The highest form of listening is through meditation. The highest form of speaking is through prayer. This energy means that it is time to expand your awareness by being open to new perspectives.

Spiritual: I communicate what I know and I know what I communicate.

The Quadrant of Dispersement
The Facts Shared

Spiritual Dispersement

Mental: This receptacle holds the energies that reach out into the environment and emanate the site's identity. It holds the energy that allows the site to be sensed from afar.

Physical: From a personal perspective, the Receptacle of Spiritual Dispersement represents the expression of your values through creative skills. This includes writing, the arts and perhaps more importantly, your vocation. It is the expression of your energy in a way that others notice while bringing you fulfillment.

Spiritual: I send what I value into the Universe and, in return, receive acceptance.

Energy Details

Mental Dispersement

Mental: This receptacle holds the energy that allows the site to perceive and be perceived. It allows all cultures to be called to the site in a way that maintains the site's identity while still bridging the cultural or environmental belief.

Physical: From a personal perspective, the Receptacle of Mental Dispersement represents the expression of your values and needs in a way other people understand. This can be accomplished through sharing your knowledge with others. Or it can be an expression of yourself in a way that helps others.

Spiritual: I express my greatest wisdom in service to everything that is around me.

Physical Dispersement

Mental: This receptacle holds the remote view of the site. It is what physical eyes first see or physical ears first hear. It also projects the site's energies in a way that calls visitors to the site. This projection also allows the visitors to use the site in a way that they understand.

Physical: From a personal perspective, the Receptacle of Physical Dispersement represents taking the elusive into a form that can be consciously understood. It involves removing blockages in order to allow understanding to come to light in a way that helps others.

Spiritual: I project my identity and receive understanding in return.

The Witness Energies

These witnesses are a mental bridge between the all knowing Universe and the physical world. A witness is like a halfway house between the spiritual world and the physical world. The witness energy provides a level of consciousness that bridges what you want with what you are ready to experience.

Note that what you want and what you are ready for are not always the same thing. These witness energy bridges, however, will always bring you closer to your goal, whether it be a change of attitude, or some more direct physical manifestation.

1 - Manifestation

Mental: The Manifestation witness is the complete process of bringing what you want into the physical world. This includes anything that is physical, mental or spiritual.

For instance, a physical want may be greater income, a new car or a job. A mental want may be clearer perception, expanded awareness, or better balance when dealing with a family issue. A spiritual want may be greater peace, more focused meditations, or enlightenment.

Physical: The Manifestation witness will bring into your consciousness whatever needs to be done for manifestation to occur in a way that doesn't interfere with your own spiritual growth. This means that manifestation will align your wants with your needs. In other words, if you want a Ferrari automobile but need a good job in order to afford it, manifestation will alert you to that fact and show you the way to the job. It may also present you with a new job with the next phone call you receive. It is therefore important to stay open minded about manifestation. This is one case where stubbornness will definitely work against you.

Spiritual: I manifest.

Energy Details

2 - Healing

Mental: The Healing witness will bring whatever is needed for wholeness into your consciousness. Healing's interaction may be instantaneous and very physical, or it may be an awakening of a conscious understanding of what is needed for wholeness to begin.

Physical: Sometimes remembering a past life experience will release blockages that bind you to dis-ease. On other occasions, balancing aggression or anger will bring healing into your life. How healing occurs is a matter of your acceptance and readiness. The Healing witness will prepare the way for complete healing to occur. Remember that all dis-ease begins in the mind, so it is the mind that leads the way to any form of healing.

Spiritual: I am healed.

3 - Questions

Mental: The Question witness brings either the answer to a question, or a refinement of the question. Answers are always nice to receive; however, sometimes the fact that there is a question implies that there is confusion. The first step toward eliminating confusion is to formulate a clear question, for a clear question brings a clear answer.

Physical: Be open to any answer you might receive. There is no substitute for the Universe's wisdom. That wisdom brings unexpected answers, or, at the very least, an unexpected realization as to what the question is really about.

Spiritual: I have the answer within me.

4 - Introspection

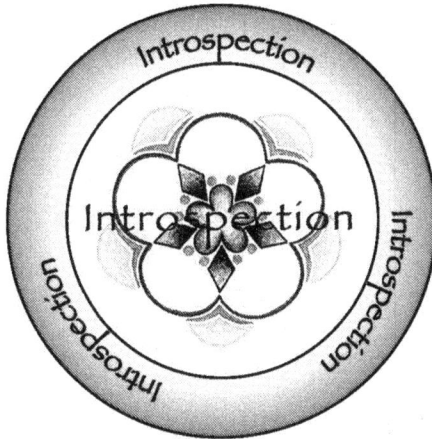

Introspection

Introspection

Introspection

Introspection

Mental: The Introspection witness brings calmness to any situation that has grown out of control. It allows a Space for truth to be seen or experienced. Sometimes introspection brings understanding. On other occasions, introspection brings the arena where understanding can be found.

Physical: Whatever the case, the introspection witness allows a look into yourself that balances. It is best to eliminate preconceived notions as to what needs to be balanced. Sometimes the unseen is the block.

Spiritual: I see, from my deepest self, who I am.

5 - Communication

Mental: The Communication witness works at many levels. It can facilitate communication between yourself and another person, between a sick pet and yourself, or between your higher consciousness and your intellectual mind. Communication, to be effective, must work at the level most needed. Be open to communication on any or all levels.

Physical: If you wish, the Communication witness can be applied to a specific level of Consciousness. Just instruct the Communication witness that you want to talk to your higher self, or your grandmother that passed away last year, or whatever your desire may be.

Spiritual: I give and I receive at all levels.

6 - Rejuvenation

Mental: The Rejuvenation witness works well for any type of healing that involves rebuilding. The rebuilding may be for a broken arm or a broken heart.

Physical: The Rejuvenation energy is depersonalized. It doesn't care what you want to rebuild, it just wants to restore something that has grown apart. It strives to restore that which was lost into something that serves the present and prepares the way to the future. This means that in order to rejuvenate a broken heart, you must first rejuvenate your attitude toward relationships.

Spiritual: I am transformed and I accept the transformation.

7 - *Peace*

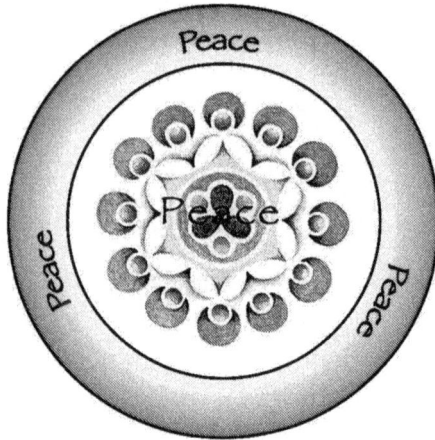

Mental: The Peace witness will create an arena of peace within yourself or within a physical space. This is a powerful witness and will always work at the level needed. All that is necessary is to be open to whatever is causing the chaos that holds off peace.

Physical: Achieving peace means that whatever is holding peace in abeyance will be removed. The Peace witness will sometimes cut out whatever is holding peace back. Peace will not come from a physical perspective; it does it from a mental or emotional perspective. To gain lasting peace, the removal of chaos needs to be made permanent. This is not done by the Peace witness; it is done through effort on your part. This means that it will often be beneficial to follow work with the Peace witness by work with the Manifestation or Rejuvenation witnesses.

Spiritual: I am peace.

The Growth Energies

Growth energies depict transformations that are necessary in order to proceed along your life path in an orderly, non-painful manner. There are five growth energies and they are meant to break you loose from a preconceived idea that is holding you back.

The Inward Funnel

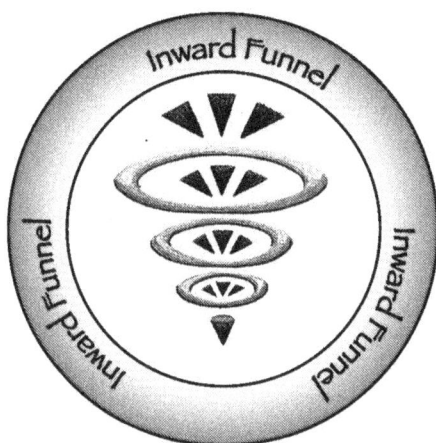

Mental: The energy of the Inward Funnel has to do with renewal from the outside in. It is an energy that can bring anything to completion if proper timing and awareness is present. It is a quiet energy that gently takes that which needs to be preserved, and brings it to a point of rest. It is almost an energy of hibernation except that what eventually emerges is rejuvenated, not expended.

Physical: From a personal perspective, the Inward Funnel represents rest and relaxation. It is the energy of a quiet vacation that involves no physical or mental activity. It represents a need to kick back and allow renewal to occur.

Spiritual: I step back into my own self and I am rejuvenated.

The Outward Funnel

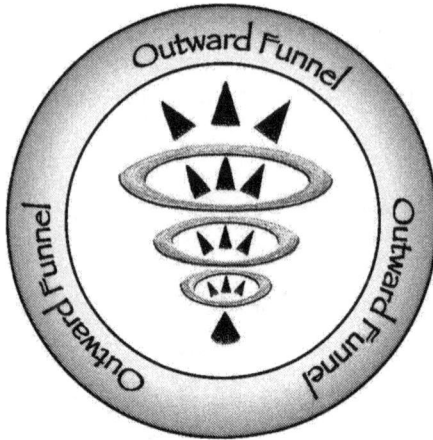

Mental: The energy of the Outward Funnel represents regeneration from the inside out. It takes a need for change, brings it to an understanding and then releases it for use. It replaces that which needs change with whatever is needed for the future. It takes that which no longer is productive and replaces it with the seed of productivity.

Physical: From a personal perspective, the energy of the Outward Funnel represents transformation starting with attitude and ending with wholeness. It places you in a state of being that allows anything to be healed, be it mental or physical.

Spiritual: I transform all within me to unequivocal acceptance of who I am.

Energy Details

The Stepping Stones

Mental: The energy of the Stepping Stones represents movement forward in a productive way. It is the next step in whatever is needed along life's path. It is not an energy that pushes but rather an energy that brings confidence.

Physical: From a personal perspective, the Stepping Stones energy represents decisive movement forward. It is time to take the next step toward the fulfilling completion of whatever you are working on or with. This is not the time to be cautious, it is time to move forward. Realize that every step in the process is important - take one step at a time.

Spiritual: I joyously take the next step.

The Seed

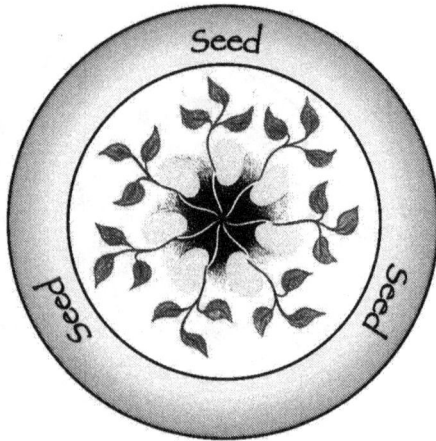

Mental: The energy of the Seed represents the germ of anything new. It is the energy of aware readiness. The energy is hidden until the timing is proper for its recognition and use.

Physical: From a personal perspective, the Seed represents the dawning of a new perspective, idea or creation. It is the small nagging felt deep within your awareness. In order for the seed to bear fruit, it must be taken into a full awareness and nurtured with respect and activity

Spiritual: I am the seed from which all grows.

Energy Details

The Bridge

Mental: The energy of the Bridge represents crossing the boundary between what is known with that which is unknown.

Physical: From a personal perspective, the Bridge energy represents a courageous leap into the unknown. It represents the desire as well as the ability to do whatever it takes to understand an issue or problem. It means that you are now ready to comprehend whatever has been puzzling.

Spiritual: I courageously look at, and then step into, the unknown.

Index

Index